WHAT'S A LADY TO DO?

WHAT'S A LADY TO DO?

by

Retha Sullivan

ISBN: 1-58820-161-9

This book is printed on acid free paper.

1stBooks - rev. 01/05/01

PREFACE

"What's a Lady to do?" is meant to be a tongue-in-cheek approach to what both sexes refer to as the unforgivable sin of adultery and betrayal, geared toward women fifty and beyond, currently living somewhere between estrogen replacement therapy and death.

The information I am about to share with you will hopefully help you to realize that the past is part of what we have become and who we are. To grow, we have no choice except to move forward. No one lives in the past.

My hope is that this book will help each of its readers to understand the male animals that we are forced to share our planet with. Women must learn to make sound decisions regarding the outcome of their furures. There are many great girls out there who believe that putting up with a liar and a cheat is better than nothing at all!

When were we forced to put a price tag on dignity and self-respect?

If and when we come to the point where we can justify lying and cheating, the road will only lead to pain… destruction will certainly follow. We must learn to believe in something beyond ourselves, otherwise we will become nothing. If there is any doubt that there is something going on in a relationship, then there is actually no doubt at all. Stop once in awhile and force yourself to take that long painful look inside. The journey will always help you to know who you are. It can possibly hurt you or it may heal you. It will be your choice, however, when you have completed the journey you will have become a more complete and contented person. There is a sharp difference between right and wrong and liars and cheaters will go to great lengths to protect themselves from receiving their just rewards. If everyone did what they knew was right, no one would be having any problems. Sometimes in life there just isn't a gray area. Something is either right or wrong.

Today or tomorrow your mate may come home and tell you that he has found someone new. He will tell you that they never meant for it to happen. It just did! You will hear him tell you that he and his new found love have so much in common! And believe me, they do! What they have in common is cheating, sneaking around, and lying.

You are married to a loser and so is her husband. Losers always seem to find each other. If this weren't true, you and your mate would not be having this conversation right now.

Every girl wants a cheater, a sneak and a liar for a husband. Every man wants a cheater, a liar and a sneak for a wife. Right? That is exactly what they have found in each other! Both are so happy to have at last found what each has been searching for all through life! Neither seems to know that the world is a much larger place then what one can hold in the palm of the hand. Nor do they realize one very basic concept: For every action there is a resulting reaction.

What will you do? How will you react?

All relationships extend beyond the home. If people do what is right at home they do what is right outside the home. What they do is a directly connected to what and who they are! One either contributes to a relationship or contaminates it! People who have nothing to hide, do not hide anything.

Cheaters and liars also never take direct responsibility for failure! They always blame someone else, the easy way out! Each day when you wake up, you and only you have two choices to make. You either do what is right or do what is wrong. Only you are responsible for your choices!

You can choose to be a victim or you can learn and take charge of your life. Life is nothing but choices. Once in awhile we are forced to choose how we are going to live our life! Every situation is a choice. How each and every one of us reacts to that situation is either a personal choice or just a reaction.

Chapter One
REALTY CHECK

Sometime, soon after you've passed the fifty mark, somewhere between estrogen replacement therapy and death, there is more than a 50 percent chance that your husband will have an affair or has already had one.

Statistics show the divorce rate in the United States is exceeding 50 percent. If a light bulb hasn't just come on in your sweet little head, girl, you'd better get with the program! Do a reality check.

I know exactly what you're thinking . . .

"My husband never! He's so busy working, when would he find the time?"

Or, "Not my man. He loves me, and he wouldn't think of it. Besides, he's home every night. Sure, sometimes he's a little late, but he always calls to let me know where he is."

Or, "On weekends he's home unless, of course, he has plans to golf , hunt or fish with his buddies. Now and then they do go for the weekend, but that's just a man thing! He and his buddies play cards and have a few drinks once in awhile."

You know what I say? *Maybe . . . maybe not!*

Everyone tells me the wife is always the last one to know. I don't believe that. If it is happening to you, face it. You know!

First off, you know something is wrong but you can't seem to put your finger on it. You ignore the signs and make excuses for him. For example, suddenly nothing you do is right. He makes offhanded remarks about the way you dress, or your hair is never combed, or your hair is the wrong color, or your hair is too short or too long . . . and the list goes on. You might say something to yourself like, "He doesn't mean to hurt my feelings. He cares about me and just wants me to stay on track." But he never puts his arms around you anymore. And the only kisses you get are the hello and maybe the oft' regarded goodbye Judas kisses on the cheek. But you say to yourself, "He's just preoccupied with his job. He's got so much on his mind."

The only conversation he initiates lately is on the weather or where the kids are. You know he's not interested in how your day went and if you ask about his day, you always get the same generic canned comment as your answer: "It was okay." If you press for more, the answers range from *nothing new going on* to even a nasty *Why do you want to know? You don't know any of those people, anyway.*

If you complain about never talking anymore, you get the standard comebacks:

"What do you want to talk about?"

Or, "What are you looking for?"

Or, "What do you want from me?"

You react! Your feelings are hurt; you say nothing, you cry, you may even start a fight. "Any kind of attention is better than none at all," you tell yourself. "Probably just his age, that male menopause phase everyone talks about. He'll snap out of it."

Yet, he doesn't.

One day, you realize he is always so busy. He says things like, "By the way, I won't be home tomorrow. Nick and I plan to golf." Or you get the "I forgot to mention it to you but a gang from work is going out tonight, so I'll be home late." There are twenty million excuses <u>not</u> to be home and I'm certain you're hearing your share, even if you aren't willing to admit it. His plans never include you. Or do they? Think about it! You feel like Mrs. Dial A. Bitch. He complains about every little thing. When is he going to snap out of this mood?

The emotional stress begins building. He hasn't touched you in months. You work off your frustrations and get angry. Now you begin to snap at everything he does wrong.

You clean the house, paint the walls, paper the bedroom, plant flowers, bake . . . anything to keep busy. You read everything you get your hands on, work crossword puzzles, go to lunch with the girls, shop and try to create a life beyond the one you exist in. You try to be happy, but your heart is aching. You try and deny how you feel inside, always thinking *no one must know.* You feel like a complete failure.

"What did I do wrong? Everyone else I know is so happy!"

You cook what he likes. But he doesn't eat that anymore. What? He's on a diet? Since when? He hasn't been home enough lately for you to know! Then he suddenly begins picking out his own clothes. Your taste he now tells you is so completely different from his and besides that, you aren't "out there!" He's thinning down and trying to dress, look and act younger. You think, *must be that male menopause thing*, so you let that go by. Once again you find yourself adjusting to something else. For thirty years he has asked for your judgement in what he picked out in clothing and you always enjoyed shopping for him and with him. But now, you find yourself behind the times and your taste is all wrong. Look around and become aware of your surroundings! Are there extra changes of clothing always in the car just in case it rains or gets chilly or, God forbid, there's a national disaster? Don't you find it strange that even the kids begin to make fun of the clothes that he or someone else is picking out? "He looks ridiculous, like some wanna be. Is he trying to compete with us or what? He's really losing it." While searching for your sunglasses in the glove compartment of the van one day, you find directions to a house on the lake in a town nearly fifty miles away. He has already told you about the plans he made to go on another golf outing for four days next Thursday. You question him about the note and the directions. At first he doesn't know how it got there, then he grabs the little yellow post-it note and swears it's your hand writing and actually spends time exaggerating his lie to the point of trying to convince you that you actually did write the note. "Remember when you were looking for that second hand freezer? Greenville is the place we went to." To avoid another confrontation, you agree. "How stupid does he think I am? I looked at that freezer in Greensburg." You know in your heart he is taking someone new with him or meeting her there. He busies himself cleaning the van. That van hasn't been cleaned that good in three years! The inside is cleaned and polished as well as the outside. He is trying to wash away any visible signs that you exist. He hasn't been so careful in cleaning a vehicle in years. You know for sure that he is trying to impress that certain someone. This is the man who would rather take a vehicle to the car wash. He's the one who for years would wash the outside and clean only the inside of a vehicle when it reached the garbage can on wheels stage. Tonight he even hides in the bathroom with his secret stash of hair color. When he emerges, he doesn't have a grey hair. Now he begins to tell you how much energy he has and doesn't want to sit around. This man has all this new found energy! There are so many things that need fixed around here, and the lawn needs mowed, however he doesn't have the time to worry himself with such mundane things. You know he is sixty years old, but in one of his two brains some easy female has convinced him that he's Mr. Wonderful. You know which brain she has convinced!

"Why Joel, we have so.....much in common, you have so much energy, you're so much fun, and you're always ready for a good time. I can hardly wait for you to make love to me each time. No one in my life has ever made me feel this way. I can hardly get through the day without seeing you. And when you tell me when we're on the phone to wear nothing at all, I always try to find an excuse to call you again or make an excuse to drive to your office so I can feel your body against mine." You know the scenario! The crap goes on and on. The strange thing is that you don't want to believe you are actually married to someone stupid enough to fall for those lines. Let me tell you: YOU ARE! Men have insane egos! If any half decent looking female blows enough smoke up their anal canal, that ego becomes so inflated brain two kicks in. When brain two takes over, that intelligent man you were so proud to be married to, turns into a lying, conniving, cheating, sneaking Dickhead. He will protect, take up for, lie, do whatever it takes to sneak around with this wonderful new found love. She can actually make him believe that he has an exclusive on her, has never done this kind of thing before, and wouldn't want to hurt anyone . . . especially his wife and family. Right! The fact is, if she is doing your husband, she is doing someone else when he's not around or she has done this many times before. If she is married, her own husband is celibate! The two of them have given up sex! Right!!! Some women just don't have the real brains it takes to get what they want any other way. There is an old saying, "If you are not

4

smart enough to get what you want, you can always seduce the boss and get it anyway." Throw it in his face enough. He'll take it sooner or later. Some women would rather have a pleasant affair with the powers that be than work to elevate themselves. It is much easier, doing something you know so well, especially if the power is married. If he is married, he has as much to lose as the female does and will keep his mouth shut, never exposing himself or her. After all, he would never want anyone to know he makes decisions based on the sexual favors he is getting from some female..

The fact remains that a man can only feel attached to a female if he is having sex with her. Every living female in the world knows this! You are having these thoughts, the signs are there, but still you are living in denial! Why would any sensible woman want a cheating jerk? The truth of the matter is that being the mistress is a lot more fun. It's all fun and games. Think about it. There is no laundry, no housework, no sleeping alone, no runny noses, no cooking, no nagging. The list goes on and on. She gets great sex, is treated like a queen, enjoys fun weekends and afternoon delights, rarely has to wait, never gets called stupid, crazy, ignorant, or a bitch, and never gets accused of always thinking she is right. The mistress never gets screamed at when she is sick or scared and never ever gets told that she is fine or to "Stop crying and get over it; you exaggerate everything. That didn't hurt you." After all, she needs him, and you are so self sufficient, according to her and now him, that you will do just fine when the time comes. Then she goes home and hops in the sack with her own husband when necessary. Oh, excuse me, I forgot that she does not have sex with her husband anymore! She has the best of both worlds!

The truth is, and every woman knows it... *ALL MEN HAVE TWO BRAINS*. Yes, two, one in the head and the other in the penis! If the penis brain is the smart part, we call this charming fellow Dickhead. A smart Dickhead operates on two sets of lies. One set he uses only when he's fully dressed. The second set is used when he's undressed. I learned years ago that a lady never, I repeat, never believes a naked man. All naked men turn into Dickheads to get their way. Remember, the same blood flows to both brains but if it reaches the lower brain first, that's the smart part of him. He cheats on his wife! One set of lies is what he operates on when he is with his wife, who now only sees him fully dressed, and the other set he operates on when he is around or with the significant other, who now sees him fully naked most of the time. When the Dickhead operates mostly on the penis brain, he becomes a real ass-hole. Women can also become ass-holes. So much for the theory: If it walks like a duck and talks like a duck, it must be a duck!

"An ass-hole is any human being that will relieve them self in their own nest. Your husband can easily fall into this category because men usually take things at face value. Men generally don't sweat the small stuff because to men most stuff is small. They tend to believe that there is more gain in being wrong than right if the wrong makes them feel good! Some animals never open their eyes for six weeks or more after they are born. There are both men and women who it takes upward of fifty years for them to open their eyes. Yet, they still are unable to see the trees because of the forest. I feel great sadness for these people. For them life is never simple.

They become just like the hajji, believing persistence gets them anything they want.

However, every once in a while that same persistence gets them a lot of things they don't want! Life is so full of surprises! The time has come for you to look out for you, and do what is best for you. Dr. Ginni Saunders, a professor of psychology, at San Francisco State University says that the body and brain together respond to love. Martain Heinstein, a professor of psychology, at San Francisco State University teaches a course on the psychology of love. He claims that you get the same high from love as you do from drugs or cigarettes. Research has indicated that women who lack the social support of love and human touches seem to have an increased circulation of fat throughout their bodies. This promotes the clogging of arteries and can trigger heart attacks. Professor Martin claims that this may seem like an all to scientific view of love or the lack thereof --but this is literally a broken heart. Remember the old Hindu proverb: " Those who give... have all things. Those who withhold...have nothing!"

When someone cheats in a relationship, the magic disappears. Some people, but very few, are able to work things out and seemingly have a well functioning marriage. The magic, however, is lost forever! It becomes part of the past. All throughout life, certain moments will trigger unwanted buried thoughts to resurface and the parties involved have no control over the times this will happen. There will be many times for these couples when questions surface in the mind of the victim even if they aren't addressed. We are only human, and reliving yesterdays in your mind, if only for a brief second, is always very painful and humiliating.

Friday night arrives again, so you think to yourself, *I'll be nice and sweet and put the moves on him. He's quiet, but that's all right. Probably got a lot on his mind and he's had such a busy week. So have I, come to think of it.*

You've cleaned, cooked, washed and ironed his clothes and yours. You've grocery shopped and done the ever so many mundane chores. You've even found yourself doing jobs around the house he should be doing, but there's no interest. He's too busy!

Women go through all the antics, plots, and schemes, knocking themselves out for what? Your other half doesn't notice, couldn't care less, has not even a vague idea why, except perhaps you must like to do those things. Right?!? He never mentions anything about the chores that get done. Does he think there's actually a grocery fairy? Brain two has him convinced that you have hired a maid that washes and irons his clothes, a painter and repair man to keep the house up, and a gardener to mow the lawn and tend the flowers. Not once does he offer to help with anything around the house, if the word work is remotely involved. He works all day while you stay home, talk on the phone, watch TV, and lounge. Why should you ever get tired? After all, the good fairies are still out there!

<u>Wrong.</u>

7

The real clincher comes much later that night. You've showered, even put on a little make-up and perfume. When your sweetie gets in bed, you roll over and give him a kiss to say good night. The first, last and only words out of his mouth are, "What's wrong with you? Are you crazy? Why don't you put some clothes or something on?" You're hurt, slink back to your side of the bed and cry yourself to sleep. Surely, no one can hurt this badly without dying! If he knows, he doesn't respond. He really doesn't care. You've been sleeping in the nude for six months now. It's more comfortable! Where has he been?!?

You are just a lonely, love-starved wife reaching out to your husband. Human spirits must connect to remain as one. In order to connect, humans must talk, touch and care! When these three little things cease, so do the three little words. You remember him, the one that took the vow with you before God to always love and cleave only unto you? You might remember, but he sure as hell hasn't! You can bet the house…. He's definitely caught a bad case of "Peckeritis[1]!" He's having sex with someone every chance he gets, but it sure as hell isn't you! Your knight in shining armor is definitely having an affair! You can't eat or you eat everything in site. You find yourself thinking terrible things about yourself and self esteem plummets quickly to the bowels of the earth.

"There's something wrong with me." He always finds an excuse or reason to avoid sex, even if it's unspoken. He never kisses you goodnight unless you kiss him to initiate contact and then he quickly rolls over with his back to you and falls asleep immediately. And, God forbid, if you mention sex. He evades the issue like you have the plague. The excuses range from a headache, had a long day and he is just too tired, or perhaps to just smiling and shrugging you off or moving out of your way. How dare you be so demanding?! In some ways men are just like women.

Get prepared for one of the two sets of lies if you pressure him. The two sets of differing lies are both constructed to

---

[1] A disease men catch when they don't understand or remember the all important three little words: "No, I'm married."

achieve the same ends as to what he wants you to believe at any given time. The rules of stability, and family values have just changed. If he still expects breakfast in bed, tell him to sleep in the kitchen! This is certain to get an interesting response!

Any woman knows how to get the undying attention of a man! Call him a few times a day. Always speak in a soft wanting voice, make him think you can't do a certain thing without his input, have no lulls in the conversation, and definitely make him feel good about himself. Say something sexy to turn him on. Never ask him to pick up bread and milk at the store! When he hangs up, he will not be able to get you out of his mind. This is an easy thing to do if you happen to work for him! All at once you will be his new best friend! Massage the ego enough and you've got yourself a lover! Life is really quite simple in the animal kingdom! I liked life better when people were more human. It seems today everyone is busy playing head games.

Remember the words that opened many episodes of the Guiding Light[2]? "There is a destiny that makes us brothers. None goes his way alone. All that we send into the lives of others comes back into our own." Sooner or later everyone will be held accountable for their actions. Not one will get out of this world unscathed.

That old saying, *He who laughs first laughs last*, still holds true. So the first rule to remember is don't ever forget to laugh, it's not so much how as to when! Laughter results in fewer wrinkles and can help get you through some of lives toughest moments.

Women over the age of fifty happen to be the fastest growing group of people living at the poverty level in America today. The fact is so astonishing that many don't realize it. It has become an accepted fact of American life. We are less sensitive as a society (less human). The norm seems to be, if I am not affected, who cares. One day, you may be the one affected, then how will you feel? Is it then that you will decide

---

[2]The Guiding Light is a soap opera on TV and is a registered trademark of the Procter and Gamble Company.

if to make the choice to become compassionate and caring or get even. Only you can make the choice to become a victim.

After the age of fifty, females in our society are still an expendable commodity. If you don't believe it, try to find employment. For one thing, your age is against you. And God help you if you've been out of the workforce for any length of time. You will find that you are either over qualified or under qualified! How dare you take twenty years off to rear a family?! Did you think you were June Cleaver?

Employers look at you as if you are totally out of your element. They silently think to themselves *she's only got five or six good years left*. This is the age of corporate downsizing and you'll find yourself competing with men and women twenty years your junior with limitless energy and the 'I'll do <u>anything</u>' attitude it takes to get that job or a one better. And I do mean 'I'll do <u>anything</u>! "Sleeping with the boss" has become the so-what statement of the ninety's. Everything depends on becoming a team player. No one is permitted to have an independent thought. If the team decides it's the in thing to sleep around and you rebel, you are off the team. Plain and simple. No one on your team dares tell you that they think you are an ass-hole! After all, all ideas must be discussed and massaged to get one common thought! After fifty, do you actually believe you can compete with some young energetic hard body that has had the latest plastic surgery techniques applied to her breasts, tummy , face and rear. Sure! Only in your dreams!

"Thank you for coming in Mrs. Smith, we'll keep you in mind," these employers say. "Right! File thirteen!" you say to yourself as you leave, knowing this was just another exercise in futility! "Screw the qualifications," you mutter out loud to yourself as you get in the car.

Every divorced woman doesn't get a raw deal. Once in awhile the shoe is on the other foot, but the stats prove most women over the age of fifty aren't getting enough to get by on from the ex-spouse. I'm sure you can cite the exception. "Look what so-and-so gets and she was the one running around!" Human nature is built upon contradictions and exceptions. But, whether you care to admit it or not, the facts remain the same.

10

For every exception there are twenty who fall into poverty and struggle daily to survive. Find out for yourself. Look into the statistics available on divorced women over the age of fifty. Or why not check with Hillary?

"There are plenty of minimum wage jobs!" everyone tells you. However, the 'everyone' telling you this, is not working for minimum wage.

When you get a divorce or find out your spouse is unfaithful, the feeling is the same as if he or she died. There is only one problem. You can not bury the spouse, collect the insurance and get on with life. Every day that he or she passes through your life you will feel the pain, if only for an instant. It will always be there. Telling the truth is supposedly and realistically the first step of all forgiveness. The problem is that a liar and a cheater[3] never tell the truth. I honestly believe they do not know or even understand the difference between truth and lies. But one must realize that to a cheater the destination is never as important as the journey. They do not think any further than the feel good moment at the time to the next feel good moment in the future. They only think about themselves. Never do they give any thought as to how their actions can or will affect or hurt the people so close in their lives, nor do they care. There isn't one thought given to wedding vows, lost respect, honesty, morals, or the person waiting at home. The one at home is the first one they will choose to blame for their actions because they must have someone to blame and never take responsibility for anything they do. It is always the fault of someone else. This is called guilt transference and a cheater becomes a pro immediately in using it.

A study from the National Cancer Institute found that women are five to eleven times more likely to develop cervical cancer if their men have many other sex partners during a marriage. According to Dr. Keerti V. Shah, a professor at John Hopkins School of Medicine, human papilloma virus, or HPV, a disease commonly spread through sexual intercourse, is a primary cause of cervical cancer. Male behavior is important.

---

[3]In marriage, a liar and a cheater are one and the same.

Men can literally take cancer home to their wives. Many women's risk for cancer increases through direct and indirect exposure, while this virus presents almost no cancer risk for men. There are more than 75 different strains of the HPV virus. Researchers have found all different types of HPV strains in genital specimens taken from husbands. There is no treatment for HPV infections, but the body's own immune system, if healthy, usually eradicates the virus within six to 18 mos. The infection can be started over and over if there is new exposure. The more exposures the greater the risk. The more sexual partners you or your partners have, increases your risk. Condoms are ineffective because these types of diseases are transmitted by intimate skin to skin contact and shed beyond protected areas. Fondling and foreplay can be very costly to someone. That someone could be you! If you are the other woman, I feel great sorrow for you knowing you can not do any better then sleep with a married man. You alone make the choice to sleep with a cheater, a loser and a liar. The only upside is the fact that you know what he is and he is not going to change. Don't kid yourself!

If he can be seduced into going to bed with you, don't think you are anyone special! You are not the first, and will not be the last. You are just EASY, entertaining, accessible, stupid, and most likely younger than his wife. Brain two has just kicked in. His wife is much better in bed than you are, but today she is busy washing and ironing his shirts. You just happen to be willing, and available for the second hand attention. Betcha he will close his eyes during intercourse! Mr. Dickhead closes his eyes to tune out his partner! It's not brain surgery. And if push comes to shove he'll put his pants on in one hell of a hurry. If his wife has half a brain, she can grab you both by the short hairs and come up smelling like a rose! Living a lie may seem blissful, but reality will intrude sooner or later. Ask yourself if denial is better than facing disappointment head on. Some of the loneliest people in the world have their man and also have someone else. We all create our own reality! It is common for people to distort or even disregard what is actually going on around them. Each of us seems to depend on preconceived opinions that were passed down during our childhood as to how things should feel and how things ought to be, according to Brad Blanton, author of "Radical Honesty: How to Transform Your Life by Telling the Truth." It is not an easy task to be honest about your motives. If you really tell the truth, often, you will find out that you are wrong. God forbid! Cheaters lie because they want other people to believe that how they interpret the relationship is right. If they are right, then they feel secure and do not have to deal with the embarrassment or shame of an affair!

If there are natural born killers, it stands to reason that there are others that are just natural born cheaters! You cannot change who they are! What you must remember is that you are not responsible for their choices. If a person has such a low opinion of them self that crawling between the sheets with someone new is what boosts their self esteem and this action makes each involved feel special instead of available and easy, one has to wonder about the intelligence of the parties involved. Don't get me wrong! Sex is here to stay, thank God. It is not a special gift exchanged by only loving married people anymore. It seems anyone can get in line. Just smile, say the right feel good words, massage an ego and hop in the sack. This is love? I think not. It is a choice!

Rhonda Jean Smith grew up in a small town in Missouri: Newton Falls. Population 13,789, the kind of town where it seemed everyone was either related, a best friend, or at the very least knew each other.

Rhonda was the only child of Irish English parents, high school cheerleader, popular and loved by everyone in the town. She was a tiny, 110 pound blonde, looking over the world with her blue eyes at five feet, two inches. She loved everyone. Her home always was filled with friends of both sexes, cooking up something special in her parent's kitchen, watching TV, sitting on the front porch playing board games or just talking and laughing. Everyone loved to visit her home and she would at times come in to find friends there waiting for her, eating mamas' famous apple pie. Her quick wit and good-natured personality were known to everyone. Even her mischievous funny pranks did not go unnoticed.

One weekend she and the girls had gone to the lake to lie in the sun. That evening C.J., a good friend of the girls, knocked on the door of the motel room and asked if they had brought anything for sunburn. Marti, Rhonda's best friend, immediately began to search for something to give him. Rhonda picked up a jar and tossed it him. "This will do the trick! C.J., your pain will be gone in a flash." C.J. thanked the girls, took the jar with him and left. When the girls returned home the next day, C.J. was waiting at Rhonda's. He looked as if he had been scalded. The skin on his face was bright red. "What did you give him to put on that burn, Ron?" Marti asked.

"The only thing we had."

"You gave me deodorant for that burn!"

"Did you use it?"

"Sure, I thought it must be a new remedy." Everyone laughed.

In 1959, for the evening graduation ceremonies at Newton High, the auditorium was so hot that Rhonda had opted to hang her new dress in the girl's locker room at the last minute. She wore only underwear under her graduation gown. Her graduation speech was not about the future; instead she had written about herself. Mama had told her to write her speech on a subject she was knowledgeable about instead of writing about things she thought she knew about. Her speech had been funny and witty as she expounded on her years at Newton High. Everyone had cheered and clapped when she was finished. As she left the podium, the bright lights shined through her long graduation gown and revealed to the town a small young girl in only panties and a bra.

Of course, Rhonda was unaware of this until her name was called to receive her diploma. Mr. Carter, the high school principal bent his head down and whispered so softly to her. " I had no idea, child, that you needed a dress for graduation. My wife and I would gladly have bought you one."

"I bought a dress sir. I loaned it to your wife to wear this evening." Rhonda laughed as she said this. The mike was up higher than either realized and everyone had heard the conversation. The audience laughed loudly and Rhonda curtsied. Mrs. Carter laughed with everyone else and just shook her head. She was a rather tall lady and outweighed Rhonda by at least sixty pounds. Marti and C.J., Rhonda's very best friends, had laughed about that incident all through college and even now, Marti would taunt her about her choice always to wear nothing at all if possible.

"So what's your point Marti," Rhonda always had asked?

Marti never did tell her!

Even now, 50 odd years later, they shared that moment and Marti always laughed!

Life had not been kind to Marti but she had learned to laugh again.

No one ever dreamed that their lives would take the turns about to transpire.

The story is fiction, of course, but taken from fact. Names, places, and events were changed to protect those involved by no choice of their own.

What follows is a story about a woman, any woman, you perhaps, struggling to make the right choices and desperately trying to beat the odds.

What a beautiful day it is, Rhonda was thinking as she finished cleaning the house. Joe and Park pulled in the driveway as she walked out onto the porch. Just then the phone rang. This phone call would change Rhonda's life forever. It would be only the beginning of many to follow.

"Is Joel there?" It was a woman's voice.

"Not yet," Rhonda answered unsuspectingly. "Do you care to leave a message?"

"No message, thank you."

Ten minutes later the phone rang again. " Mrs. Smith, you may as well know that I am sleeping with your husband and I usually get what I want! For now, I have decided I want him. He was supposed to meet me after work today. If you think you can out smart me, don't try. Even if you tell him about this call, he will never believe you. I already have him convinced that I would never do anything to hurt you or his family and he believes everything I tell him. He actually thinks I need him and you don't. Even if you can get him to admit that he has a special friend... he will never believe that I would call you, and furthermore, he will tell you that I am no threat to you. He tells me that your marriage has been over for a long time so I am not the one to blame. I have him convinced that he can't live without me. We never meant this to happen; we just clicked. We have so much in common. I suggest you find yourself someone else. Bye now!" This woman quickly rambled on and on , just stopped and hung up. Rhonda was stunned. The blood had rushed to her head. Tears were streaming down her cheeks and it took every ounce of energy she could muster just to hang up the phone. Joe and Park came into the kitchen and immediately knew whatever had transpired on the phone had upset her. She was so upset it took an eternity for her to tell them what had just happened. "It could be just a prank call mom," they both spoke at the same time.

When Joel arrived home that evening, Rhonda told him about the phone call and he had laughed. "Lots of people hate me Ron, it could be anyone," he said, trying to explain it away.

The calls became more frequent as time went on.

Now the boys were getting calls at work giving them information about their dad. It seemed everyone knew except Rhonda and the boys. Phone calls began to come from Joel's so called friends, people he worked with, and from men in his golf league. Finally, he did admit to Rhonda that there was someone else in his life now, but she would never do anything to hurt her or the boys. Yes, she was married also, however, she was not a threat to anyone. She needed him! The words came back in her face almost verbatim, as to what that woman had told her only a few weeks back. Joel always referred to the woman as she or her. Didn't she have a name? "It's most likely the girl I was seeing before she came along that's calling you," he had said ever so smugly, "I got rid of her when she started to get too serious." He acted so proud of this fact! "I don't feel guilty either, so don't try and go there, I'm not your son. You may as well get used to it and know that I plan to do whatever makes me feel good, Rhonda. If you have a problem with that, then it's your problem. The only thing you're worried about is the fact that you will be alone! Besides, this one is a better lay than you, she sure knows what to do in the sack!" "I only know what you taught me, unfortunately". Rhonda had managed to say becoming hysterical and left the house. She managed to call the boys from her car phone to meet her at her mothers. They arrived at almost the same time to find their mother inside talking and crying to their grandmother.

" I don't know what to do . . . I don't know what to do. I would like to kill him and her both. How could he do such a demeaning thing to me? How could he embarrass the boys, and humiliate us this way? His choices have destroyed this family! I loathe the sight of him!"

"When you don't know what to do, do nothing," Mama quietly said to Rhonda. Mama had always been the pillar of strength for the whole family. Rhonda was ready to kill and would not be quieted down. Tears welled in the boys eyes. They had never witnessed such hurt and rage in their mother before. "I wish he was dead!"

Rhonda sat fidgeting, eyes red and swollen, hugging her two grown sons, knowing they needed her love and support. They clung to her side, trying to console her, not knowing how to but trying to relieve her and themselves of the pain that had so easily and casually been inflicted by their father.

Joe and Park had recovered from an almost fatal car wreck only a year ago. She had gotten the call early that summer morning. The boys had been on their way to mow a lawn when their vehicle had been struck broadside by an oncoming van. Joel had not as yet left for work and immediately went to the scene of the accident. Both boys had been transported to the hospital by ambulance. When Joel arrived back at home to pick up Rhonda, all the color had been drained from his face. He looked as if someone had shot him.

"Are they dead?" she had screamed.

He had shaken his head at the same time saying, "No, they are badly injured."

When Joel and Rhonda arrived at the hospital, they were getting ready to transport Joe to a trauma unit in a nearby town. Rhonda talked to Park thinking that he was only very shook up. As it turned out, Park was bleeding to death from a ruptured spleen. When Rhonda arrived at the trauma unit with Joe, he was immediately taken into surgery for a broken pelvic bone and broken clavicle. She was later informed he also had damage to the eye socket and closed head injuries. She called her mother thinking that Joel would take Park there and come to the hospital. When they had not arrived, she knew something had gone wrong. Joel's call came in an instant later. Park was in the O.R. in surgery at the same time Joe was. It was a nightmare that every parent hopes to never endure. No one even knew if either boy would make it through the night. It had taken many prayers and a long healing period. But God had seen them through this. How could anyone ever look at those boys again without thinking of the miracle God had given to them and their parents. Both had made a full recovery. What a Gift! God is ever merciful! How dare Joel take so much for granted from God!! How could he so easily give up the gifts God had given? Joel was not a stupid man. He surely knew that what he was doing would cost him the love and respect of his children, to say the least. They adored both their mother and father and were having a very difficult time handling the situation at hand.

"We're so sorry, Mom," Park said compassionately, the tears falling from his eyes.

"How can he do this to us?" Joe asked through the tears. "We're his family! When you're little, you can learn to call anyone that loves and cares for you 'Mom and Dad.' I never want to even be in the same room with that pig of his!" "Now Joe…wait a min…. Rhonda did not get to finish her sentence.

"He's right, Mom. For twenty years Dad preached right and wrong to us. What about the rules for himself? Or has he always had two sets, one for himself and another for us? You don't deserve this, and we're ashamed of him."

"He's still your father," Rhonda said, trying to control the anger and hurt. "I always felt that he loved you both, as much as he could love anyone, and I can't imagine why he would do anything to really hurt either of you. He's lost all of our respect, and doesn't even realize it. He does need your love."

"Mom! Get real!" Joe yelled. "How can you love someone who sneaks around breaking up our family? Are you asking us to love someone we can not trust? You of all people know better and have taught us better than that."

"Dad always said, 'Be a man! Never sneak or lie; always tell the truth. Be honest. Only you face that man in the mirror every morning. You have to face yourself!' What a fucking hypocrite!" With that, Park, who was almost screaming and trying to control his feelings, stomped toward the kitchen like a small beaten child. His large frame for twenty-two suddenly seemed so fragile.

"Everything became dispensable for Dad!" Joe quietly murmured. "Remember when I was dating Sandy, Mom? He had a royal fit because she was only separated from her husband. 'There are just some things *you don't do*, Joe!' Right, Dad. But it's all right for you? I should ask him that!" Joe can't hold back the tears, but he rambles on. "The man I called 'Dad' for twenty-four years pulled the rug out from under everything he ever tried to teach me. He's not that special person I always looked up to anymore. He's just like everyone else's father that runs around. What happened to "Be an example, Joe?!" What a joke! Now I guess the rules are do as I say not as I do' You know if we say anything, he'll tell us to get out. I can hear it now. This has nothing to do with Park or me. Right! He'll be certain to tell us that!" That's what every person wants in life alright, either a whore for a mother or if you can't have that to have a whoremaster for a dad! Yep, What every one dies for, the all American family!"

"His choices have infected this whole family! It's a virus of mistrust. He has no self respect!" Park had now re-entered the room as he yelled in anger. "How can he not be able to control himself and still go around thinking he can make sound decisions for us? He doesn't give a shit about any of us. Whom does <u>he</u> face in the mirror every morning? Or is that mirror so steamed up he refuses to even look?"

Rhonda was so upset. She barely had the strength to put her arms around her two grown sons. Frantically, the three reached for each other and cried. She felt for the first time in her life that she could not comfort her children, nor they her. Each one was grieving in their own private Hell, asking the same questions, *What did I do so wrong? How could he? Why? Each was* busy throwing this rotting garbage into the corners of the mind where it could fester in the dark.

She knew how deeply the boys were wounded. She and she alone, could feel their pain. "Please, Lord, don't let them waste their wounds like their father has," she silently prayed. "Every time a wound is wasted a light goes out in Heaven. When will this Angel of Darkness leave my door?"

"We love you, Mom, and we're so sorry," they both said, not knowing what else to say or how to comfort her. Trying to apologize for something they had no control over at all. Thinking somehow, they could ease her pain. Her thoughts were of how much he had managed to hurt the only three people in the world that would have always stood by him. She could see the hurt in her sons' eyes, and as only a mother can detect, she felt the hate and rage swelling inside of them.

Rage as well was swelling in Rhonda's chest. She could hardly breathe. "Go out with your friends," she said. "I'll be all right." She spoke the lie, knowing in her heart all the while that she would never be the same again. Joel had changed the course of their lives without even knowing it or ever giving any thought to it.

After the boys had left, Rhonda's aging mother, who was wise beyond her years, kissed her only daughter. She spoke firmly, but calmly. "Hold steady, Rhonda. He's not the first and won't be the last. Pray for God's guidance. Pray for him! God never said everything would be easy. He said that with him all things are possible! So I would advise you to feed your spirit and starve all of your doubts to death. Pray, Rhonda! It's the only way you will get the guidance to make the right decisions as to what is best for you and the boys."

"How can you say that to me?" Rhonda screamed back through the tears. "You can't understand the hurt. Remember when Daddy died five years ago? You at least knew he loved you and you've been going through the normal grieving process. He left you everything and you can get on with your life contentedly, with minimal problems and wonderful memories."

"Love is an action," her mother retorted. "Read Matthew 5:45[4]. Don't hate, Rhonda. Trust God to help you through this. It rains on the just as well as on the unjust and everything has a price. You are not responsible for Joel's actions! Only he is! Don't let this change who you are. Be strong. Be strong for the boys."

"I love you, Mom," Rhonda stated flatly as she was getting on her jacket to leave. "He killed the girl you loved and he's dead as far as I'm concerned. Know what hurts? I can't even bury that son-of-a-bitch because he comes through the door every night."

Mamas' voice was soft and soothing, like a warm blanket on the coldest of winter nights. "Don't let him make you bitter. It will only hurt you and there's been enough hurt. He's hurt all of you by his choices and one day he will have to face it. My only hope is that you and the boys will be around to help him through it. You are the most important people in his life. Rhonda, honey, sometimes men lose their way. People can get so caught up with their own wants that they never give a thought to who might get hurt or even care. Everything one does has a price, but I've found out through the years that seldom are they willing to pay it when push comes to shove. And once in awhile, with forgiveness, prayer and God, they do find their way back home. I hope it won't be too late, if he ever realizes what he has done. Lean on God. Without him, you are not strong enough to make this journey. Vengeance belongs to God, so pray for the boys and him."

As Rhonda drove home that dark and lonely night, one of many that would follow, her mind raced with thoughts of suicide. "My life is virtually over anyway," she told herself. "I

---

[4]That ye may be the children of your Father which is in Heaven: for He maketh His sun to rise on the evil and on the good, and sendeth rain on the just and on the unjust.

should just run this car over the bridge, that way it would appear to be an accident, or maybe I should take all of my sleeping pills at one time. Better yet, I will just take one of the penicillin tablets that Joel has in the medicine cabinet. It won't be messy and everyone will think that I just died in my sleep."! Rhonda had never forgotten the episode of anaphylactic shock that had occurred when she had taken that medication before. She had almost died then. The doctors had told her the next time she took it, she would not be so lucky, therefore, always to inform any physician of this allergy and to get a medic alert tag to wear in case of an accident when she could not speak for herself. *Please Lord*, she prayed silently, *I'm not strong enough to live with both the physical pain and the emotional pain I am expected to endure. Where are you in the grand scheme of things? I need help now! The pain of death seems so much easier to endure than the pain of living!* No one knew her secret . . . not even Joel! She had kept it to herself, trying to protect everyone she loved. *I'll handle it on my* own. She had decided two years prior. *Let everyone be happy; there will be sadness soon enough.* She had prayed and prayed! The medications had been controlling the pain thus far and she had gained weight. Surely that was a good sign! She had tried to tell Joel, but he always tuned her out only half listening. She had decided a very long time ago that he never thought anything she had to say was very important.

A morning in January, that morning when Dr. Oliver had told her about the cancer, was as fresh in her mind as if it was yesterday. He had put his hand on her shoulder and slowly began to speak. "How are you feeling today?" Not giving her time to answer he picked up the test results and began again. "The results came back positive, Rhonda. You do have cancer, just as we suspected. If you would like to see the films, I will show you exactly where the cancer is," his voice trailing off.

After that, everything in Rhonda's mind was just a blur. She could remember looking at the films and asking him how long she had to live and about the treatments, however, she didn't remember anything he had told her except that most people live about one to three years. With the great strides being made in the medical field lately… perhaps she would be more fortunate. She had left his office that day feeling totally helpless. How would Joel and the boys and mama ever cope?

"Well, girl, no one gets guarantees in life," she cried out loud, her anger and frustration building to a scream. "What have I done to deserve all this pain, God?! Why am I here? Why don't you let me die? I do not want to be a chosen woman." Then she added softly after several moments of silence, "My life is over. Joel's already found my replacement! Why would you permit this to happen? Don't I have my share already? How much is one person supposed to deal with? Why doesn't Joel and his wonderful friend have to deal with anything except the problems they make for themselves?"

That night Rhonda prayed but she didn't read Matthew 5:45. She prayed the same prayer every lady in the universe prays when she finds out her husband has Peckeritis and is an unfaithful bastard.

"It's just me again, Lord. Can't you cut me some slack, here? You and I both know he's not Mr. Wonderful. For more than twenty years I've been Mrs. Golf Widow in the spring and summer, edged out by football and television in the fall and winter. I've reheated dinners, washed, ironed, painted, papered, cleaned and spent many hours with our two sons alone. I've put up with erratic work schedules, late meetings and an occasional drunk. I'm not the worst wife in the world. Everyone knows I'm not June Cleaver, but I always tried to do the best I knew how! So if you will permit me, God, I would like to make a suggestion. Don't let him die. You can perform miracles, I know, so how about a small one! Make him humble. How about you zap his penis with dry rot. Each day it could shrivel up a little more until it's almost no longer there. Leave him only enough to void with because I can't afford Depends, although I must admit I'm having a tough time perishing the thought of him having a chapped derriere. If he's soggy, I bet the women he sleeps with won't think he's so wonderful! I've heard, Lord that every dog is entitled to one free bite, so consider this one mine.! Please help my sons cope, Help me. Please help us to know what is the right thing to do."

23

As Rhonda prayed, calmness came over her. "She thinks he is so, so Wonderful! We'll see about that! So my marriage is over? I wonder if he was seeing her or someone else when I tried to tell him how unhappy I was because he was never around and never could find the time to talk to me. I wonder if one day she will feel the emptiness in her life because he is ignoring her for someone else. Everything and everyone else always came first. I was busy cooking dinners, chauffeuring kids and listening to their problems. Mr. Wonderful claimed to be a family man, but everything else always came first . . . business, work, golf, football, weekend golf outings. People only do to you exactly what you let them do! Well guess what world? A new player is now taking to the playing field!"

And with that, Rhonda finally managed a smile through her veil of tears.

Chapter Two

"That jerk I'm married to has his nerve," Rhonda is telling Marti while she's getting her hair cut. "He kills me emotionally, destroys his family and has the audacity to expect his life to go on normally. Can you believe he expects me to cook his meals, launder his grimy clothes and let him sleep in my bed? I'm supposed to be happy and laugh! Ask no questions! Ignore everything! He says he'll let me know when he wants a divorce. Is he insane?"

"They're all ass holes," Marti retorted. "After fifty they all suffer from penis envy. If she's less than forty-five and doesn't move or complain, he'll screw her for sure. Mine did."

"You're right! The only thing that will prevent Joel from doing it is if he has to take the time to tie a board to his ass so he won't fall in." With that they both laughed.

"What are you going to do, Rhonda?"

"I plan to play their game and win. No one remembers a loser." Her blue eyes looked cold, betraying her inner thoughts, however her voice sounded as if she was only joking. "There's only one difference between a lady and a whore. A whore will, but a lady won't! A lady will use only moral and intelligent strategies as a means to get what she wants, but a whore uses only the trade she has so carefully practiced every chance she gets. She simply is very lacking in the brain department and can't get a man any other way. The only thing she knows is that a man has to have sex with a woman to feel attached. That is something every living female knows before they even hit thirty. Why do you think so many men fall for whores and it only lasts a few years, or vice versa, depending on who's shoes you're in?"

"You know, Mike's on his third marriage since our divorce, and I hear he's still running around. I saw him the other day and didn't recognize him. You know what? I don't even hate him anymore. I feel sorry for what he did to his life. The women he chose have managed to go through everything he had. He dresses like a bum, drives a clunker and spends his time with his woman at the local bars. Some life for a man his age, he's the

25

real loser. Our daughters have nothing to do with him. He doesn't even know what he gave up and for what, the sexual experience of a lifetime? I sure hope he thinks it was worth it in the end. Don't give up everything like I did. It's tough starting over. Get all you can and more. I've had to work hard to make a living for myself and my girls. The courts aren't always as fair as they should be. Did you know that Mike cleaned out our life savings and cashed every bond we had before he left? Then the bastard left us with a house payment, car payment and medical bills. The support I was supposed to get for the girls never materialized! The whole system is a joke! The toughest part is constantly finding the money for hospitalization now. And you, will never get someone to insure you at a reasonable rate now! I'm telling you, don't even think about the love or emotional support. Play it smart! Get to the money and assets first. Outsmart the Dickhead out of his assets while he is taking care or her assets!"

"Don't worry, Marti. I plan to be good to myself; Joel won't know what hit him! The tragic thing is he's been married to me for twenty-nine years and he's never taken the time to find out who I am. I honestly think, when he finds out just how smart I am, it is going to scare him to death. You know, I hated him when I found out for sure. I pray for him every night and I really don't hate him any more. The feelings I have are more of sorrow and pity! Strange isn't it, how someone you once loved can do things that hurt you so much. I can't believe that he devalued life, family, and love so much, when it is all such a fragile commodity. I'm determined to be a bigger threat to both of them than either could ever fathom! My emotions are healing slowly I think, nonetheless, I may as well get as much as I can while I can. My sons deserve to get what is rightly theirs when we both have gone to dirt city. God can see the whole picture and I am hopeful that the part I see is for a constructive purpose. Hopefully, I can do what I know is right in my heart. I may not get the chance to retake this test as you know!" With that, Ronnie smiled at Marti and Marti for an instant wondered if she was only teasing or testing the water. Ronnie never really cared what other people thought of her if in her heart she knew that she was on target. Marti smiled back, however, she knew Ronnie would never give up without a fight. For a split second, she almost felt sorry for the people involved. No one knew Ronnie like she did!

"You've gotten so thin, Rhonda. I worry about you. Are you sure you're going to be okay?"

"Truthfully, most days I feel like a piece of shit. Useless, unwanted, undesirable, disposable and depressed. I cry a lot and sleep very little. I even contemplate suicide, crazy as it sounds! I hate my life and what it has become through no choice of my own. Mostly I hate what my life has been dissolved to. But I'm still hanging' in there. Why? I don't even know. What do you do when the most important person in your life replaces you? I feel like a loose cannon! I sometimes think death might have been easier to handle. I just don't understand people anymore. No one really cares about anyone else when you get right down to it. Vows spoken before God have suddenly become only words for the moment, subject to be withdrawn when the person that speaks them has a sudden change of heart. People like that have no feelings for anyone except themselves anyway. Just think Marti. I could solve the unemployment problems in a flash!" With that, Rhonda smiled, leaving Marti to her own thoughts. What did she mean by that? She wouldn't kill him, Marti hoped. What was her fragile friend planning? She knew that she would be the first to know when things started to happen. Newton Falls was certainly going to be a happening place before Rhonda Smith was finished. All the gossip mongers would have the story of their lives to rehash over and over. Issues would be clouded more and more as the story was passed from one to another. Every one would have something to add and have the perfect solution. In the end, Ronnie would not care what they said or to whom they said it. That's the way she always was.

"Call me later. I'm going to see an attorney. I have a lot of things to take care of, while I still can." Rhonda turned to leave, intent on finishing her day's agenda.

Marti pondered the last words Rhonda had spoken as she left the shop. The fact that Joel was running around had not only

27

shocked her, but had also caused a lot of hurtful memories to resurface, things she thought had been buried and long forgotten in her life. Marti understood the pain because she had walked in those same shoes only five years ago. Everything Rhonda was telling her about Joel sounded the same as when Mike had used on them her. She remembered the horrid emotional feelings of pain and the moments that she had pondered suicide herself. Only someone who had been in that deep dark hole once could truly understand what Rhonda was experiencing.

"A lady can always smell a whore," Marti had told her friend, "no matter how she dresses, or how impeccable her manners are, a lady knows! It's just something innate in a lady. Call it the seventh sense, like smelling a rat. A lady can become a whore, but a whore can never become a lady no matter where you take her or what you put on her. She is what she is. In my book, any woman that pursues a married man or consents to sex with a married man is a whore. He's going to try and pull the guilt trip routine on you, Rhonda. Mike almost had me believing it was my fault he cheated on me. Men can justify anything when someone is pulling them around by their crotch. I know how you feel; everyone needs to feel wanted and loved. Life can surely be a bitch! I never thought Joel, of all people, would turn into an ass-hole[5]. It has taken me a long time to realize that people who aren't the smartest one's on the block are still able to justify anything that makes them feel good. They never run out of excuses."

"Let me know if you talk to Angie. Secretaries always know when things are going on. She will probably be relieved to know that the prince was a frog after all!" Marti laughed.

Rhonda listened to Marti and knew her friend would not knowingly let her make wrong decisions, but Joel had wounded her so deeply she knew in her heart the hurt would never ever go away. She felt like she was treading water in a whirlpool and would never get out. The empty feeling inside surely couldn't last forever. Or would it?

---

[5] Any man that shits in his own nest.

I've just got to focus on what's best for me, Rhonda thought. *Piss on Joel! I've got to get over the hurt, get mad, get even, whatever it takes. In my condition, from now on I'm first darling, even before thee. I'm going to be just like him. Plenty of his friends have propositioned me in the past, but being the stupid ever-faithful wife, I always said no. I wonder which part of 'no' he doesn't understand: the 'n' or the 'o.'*

Now Rhonda was getting mad. By the time she reached home, she was ready to kill. Instead of going directly into the house, she searched Joel's car and came up with names marked with stars beside them in a personal phone book. "Focus! Focus! Get tunnel vision! Burn their asses!" Having worked as a paralegal part time when the boys were in high-school had enabled her to learn a wealth of information that would now come in handy. She had been privy to certain information in other similar situations that would pay big dividends now if she could only keep her mind clear.

"Some things never change," she laughed to herself. "The best piece of ass gets the biggest star beside her name, just like before." This time, it would be different! In the past she had always turned her head the other way, ignoring the facts, thinking things would somehow be like they used to be. How stupid she had been! Stay for the kids. What would everyone think of her?

"Thank you Lord, for giving me the strength. It has only taken me some fifty odd years to realize that the desire to be wanted is second only to the desire to survive, and I always prided myself on how smart I was." A Bible verse popped into her mind just then from John 17. *Greater is he that is in you [Jesus] than he that is the world [Satan].* She searched in silence. The trunk yielded cute little empty gift bags covered with bears marked for his eyes only, faxes he couldn't bear to destroy and all sorts of trinkets only a wife would know were out of character for a sixty-year-old man like Joel to have in his car. When you live with a man for so long it seems you are the only one who knows him better than he knows himself. It's a woman thing . . . unexplainable but real. When things are out of character, you can just feel it. Joel loved gifts and was always a

29

saver. There's no fool like an old fool, so the saying goes. Joel was about to find out that true love doesn't always travel over calm water. The number one reason for divorce is adultery so give both of them enough rope and they will hang themselves. Now it was time to take action and Rhonda knew it. She could feel it.

"Well, Joel," she said aloud. "You make your choices and you live by the choices you make. But I'm making choices too. I'll bury you in your own shit. I might be sick, but I'll beat the cancer and I'll beat you at your own game."

A verse from the Bible came into her head, which calmed her for a few minutes. *If you add no fuel to the fire, the fire goes out.* But she discontinued the thought as quickly as it came and stomped into the house, ready for war.

Rhonda was at nerves end. Her hands were shaking so much she had to dial the number twice to reach the attorney's office. "Hi, Chris. This is Rhonda Smith," she said, trying to sound calm. "Any chance I can get in to see Peter today? Yes, it's urgent! Joel's cheating on me and I want to file for a divorce."

"Are you sure you want to talk to Peter?" Chris asked quietly. "He and Joel have been friends for years."

"Yes, I do, Chris. You and I both know that any attorney I have a divorce consultation with cannot represent Joel, so I'm consulting every top divorce attorney in this county and the adjoining counties. I'm starting with Peter. I want him to hear it from me. Three o'clock is fine. Joel's golfing today. I told him that I was going to see an attorney. I just didn't tell him how many or who. It's called protect thine own 'ass'ets, isn't it?"

With that, Rhonda hung up the phone. She now had regained her composure and called five other attorneys, made appointments, and then called her friend, Nora. Nora's sister-in-law worked for an attorney in the next county and could give her the names of the best ones there. Having completed the chore, she pulled out the copier and copied his personal phone book, took pictures of the pages and his little trinkets, then hid them and replaced the book. She smiled to herself as the copy machine was running. Joel had insisted she needed this machine when she was working part time. He had convinced her it would save time when she needed copies of papers that needed to be duplicated at work. " It will give you more time at home".

Rhonda was getting tired by this time. The pain was resurfacing its ugly head. She would try to do at least one load of laundry before her three o'clock appointment with Peter.

As she placed the laundry in the washer, her thoughts traveled back to an evening last week when she was doing a load of Joel's clothes. His clothes were now kept separately in his own hamper in the laundry room. "I'll wash your filthy germy clothes," she had told him, "but I better not catch any diseases from Her......the whore I mean."

"It's too late!" Joel had retorted, laughing in her face. "I dumped the last one for her because she's better in bed and you didn't even know about it. Besides she's not the only one I do. I lie to her too, but she loves me and believes me!"

"You're not the only one she's doing either, sweetie! Get a life! You're an ass-hole in love with a whore," Rhonda smugly screamed. "I'm married to the king of the ass-holes, Joel, and that's no one but you."

"You're married to me whether you like it or not! She does not think of herself as a whore and neither do I!" " Well what is she, Joel? What is she? Do you think of her as a pious innocent?" She doesn't even rate a name in this house! What am I supposed to call her? Queenie? Or shall we refer to her as the Feel Good Fairy? What about Twit? Your call big fella!

I certainly am married to you! Unfortunately someone is going to find out just how married you are, even if it is in name only. You can't even take care of what you have at home! The only thing that's going to change for you is the face across the table. One day she'll be running on you because you are both cut from the same mold! I hope I am alive to watch the show! You'll find out, Joel, sometimes you're better to live with the devil you know than the devil you don't. From now on you can do your own washing and ironing. Why should I do all the dirty work while she has all the fun?" With that, Joel stomped out of the house, jumped in the 'pecker mobile[6] and was gone for the evening. She knew his golf clubs would never be out of the bag. The only things banging balls would be Joel and Cassie or Jan or Cindy . . . whichever one was available. Rhonda knew Joel lied to her about almost everything. But one thing always rang true. He could not lie to her about his conquests. He had an ego bigger than life itself and was very proud of the fact that he had bedded more women then men half his age could hope to. Rhonda needn't be psychic to know where he would take his wounded ego to be coddled. Some things just don't change. Dogs always seek their own vomit!

She laughed to herself and hoped God had a small chuckle when he had listened to the prayer she thought that night in the laundry room.

It's just me again, Lord. I read Erica Jong many years ago, and it's not that I have a fear of flying, but I've developed this fear of falling. I've tried crawling up on the washer during rinse and spin. I've closed my eyes and tried to think of pleasant thoughts about Yanni and Superman until the spin cycle has completed. But I'm fifty-five now, and you know, I'm not as agile as Charlie's Angels. I'm afraid I'm going to fall off one of these days and break my neck. Just how far is one required to carry this faithful business? No need to answer, Lord. I just wondered, what's a lady to do?

---

[6] A name Rhonda had dubbed the van because the new license plate began with the letters PEC, and she had envisioned what had gone on in it.

Chapter Three

At 3:00 P.M. sharp, Rhonda marched into Peter's office.

"Rhonda. How are you?" Pete flashed his famous smile. He watched closely as Rhonda pulled a chair up to the oversized desk that had once belonged to his father. His father had always been a quiet man, tall and dark with a commanding presence. He was always the first to help, and the last to leave in a crisis. Everyone loved Pete Sr.

Peter had the same smile as his Dad but had not inherited his father's commanding presence. Rhonda found him to be more condescending than his dad, and seemingly practiced his craft with much less conviction. He really tried to use his smile to get around things much more so then his brains. Unfortunately, most of the time he managed to pull that off. He had the same dark hair and dark brown eyes as his father, unfortunately, they did not have the sparkle that only comes from inside, something his father would always be remembered for.

"I want a divorce, Peter," Rhonda said, as if ordering a hamburger at McDonald's. "So get out your legal pad and start writing."

"Nora called me, and I can't believe this. Not Joel, there must be a mistake. He's always been so level-headed . . . a real family man! Everyone has always envied him . . . silently of course. He had it all! A nice home, a good wife, great kids. What the hell's going on? Is he crazy?" Pete asked almost shouting. "Are you sure this is what you want?"

"No, Pete, but my choices are limited. I can't have him shot at sunrise, now can I? These are the papers you need regarding finances and assets, so what can I get?" The list of papers consisted of all assets, bills, retirement, personal belongings, collectibles, car titles, bank records, real estate holdings, bonds, jewelry and she had even taken copies of his income taxes for the last three years.

"Now, with no fault in place, you can get 50 percent, but I can't guarantee hospitalization. I'll fill out the papers if you're sure," he said quietly.

"What about the house and his retirement?"

"No judge in the land will make you leave that house after twenty-nine years," he said flatly, "and you can take half of his retirement by law if you choose to do so, in one lump sum. If you transfer it to an IRA electronically instead of taking a check, you probably won't even have to pay the tax on it. That's 50 percent on all visible assets."

"Possession is nine tenths of the law, isn't it?" Rhonda wondered out loud. She had a mischievous look as she made the statement.

"Sure," Pete said, "but I'm not going to tell you to take the valuables out."

"That's okay Peter," Rhonda said, smiling. "You know I'll do whatever I want to anyway. Oh, by the way, I want a court trial divorce. There will be no negotiating on that. It's my right and I plan to exercise it. Also, I'm going to charge the current and prior two women with indignities. Everybody will be happy when I'm done. Don't you agree?" Pete ignored her and kept on writing.

"Anything else you want in these papers?" Pete asked, changing the subject.

Rhonda looked them over and changed the support/alimony amount to a larger figure. *Peter was always conservative*, she thought to herself. She signed her name and told Peter to put a hold on having Joel served. She needed time and would let him know when. He didn't question her. He had no idea that she was a woman on a mission.

During the next two weeks that followed, Rhonda went through the same procedure with every top divorce attorney in both counties, with Nora's help, of course.

She finally made a decision on which attorney would be the best choice after all. *Pete will be shattered*, she thought, *but this way, he can't represent Joel either, and hopefully, they can remain friends. Joel could really use a friend in his life, not the kind he has now, but someone genuine, someone honest and truthful, not someone who will blow smoke up his ass to massage his ego.* Rhonda still felt pity for Joel! She was angry and going to take control of her own life but he was still a human being and the father of her children. She recalled an article in Ann Landers column years ago and it brought a chuckle to her. It seems that when the Lord made the world, he called Man aside and bestowed upon him 20 years of normal sex life. Man was angry with our creator because he had given the monkey , the lion, and the donkey the exact same time. Each creature stated that they needed only 10 of those years. Man spoke up immediately and asked if he could have the ten years left by each creature thus called. The creator and the creatures all agreed to let man have the l0 years each did not need or want. This explains why men have 20 years of normal sex, 10 years of monkeying around, 10 years of lion about it and ten years of making a jack ass out of himself.

Rhonda wondered if what Joel got out of his affairs was worth what he had lost. She wondered if he would ever have the nerve to ask himself that question and answer it truthfully. She vowed to tell him sometime in the future that when trust is destroyed, nothing can take its place. She knew he would only laugh in her face, but now she didn't care. He could not hurt her any more. She had become numb when it came to feeling anything when he spoke to her.

The attorney that Rhonda decided on was K. Stephan Sawyer. He was blonde, muscular, in his mid-forties and just happened to be a former federal prosecutor. She had talked to Nora who had assured her that he was a real ball buster in court, just what the doctor ordered. His father had cheated on his mother when he was a teenager. This had a great impact on his life, and although Nora didn't go into it, she had said he was the only lawyer around that would do whatever he felt was necessary for her to get what she needed and not reduce her lifestyle. When she called him, he had been very precise in what she needed to bring in. He spoke in a most soothing voice and was ever so polite.

"I need you to bring papers on all bank assets, debts, savings, bonds, stock, car mileage, year and title, house mortgage and appraisal, insurance policies, retirement papers and wage statements, and all taxes from last year. I am looking forward to meeting you. If you need me before your appointment, please do not hesitate to call me!"

Rhonda sat in the chair across from Sawyer, calmly watching the lawyer copy everything she had taken to his office. He ran figures on his calculator, jotting down what he deemed necessary.

"Anything else I need to know, Mrs. Smith?"

Without thinking, Rhonda blurted out, "Yes, I have cancer. Is that pertinent?"

This was the first time she had actually said the word out loud and it was to a complete stranger.

"It is certainly pertinent," he said without smiling. "How old did you say, Mr. Smith is?"

"Sixty and counting," Rhonda tried smiling.

"And you are?"

"Fifty-five," Rhonda didn't let him finish.

"Is there anything else, Mrs. Smith?" he said.

"Yes," Rhonda replied. "First, please call me Rhonda. Mrs. Smith makes me feel like an old lady."

"Fine. Rhonda it is."

"Second, I want a court trial."

"Not a problem."

"And third, I want to file charges against the females involved, for indignities. I know there is no statute of limitations on that!"

"You've done some homework, haven't you, Rhonda?" He flashed a smile. "Does your husband know you have cancer?"

"Not yet," Rhonda replied flatly.

"How many women do you want to file charges against?" he asked, leaning back in his chair, exuding confidence and control.

"Only these three," Rhonda said, passing a copy of Joel's phone book with the names starred. "These are the latest ones. The names have stars beside them. The biggest star is the best actress, the best in the sack, as he would say! There are most likely others. I am assuming that these three are the latest pigeons."

"Where did you get this?" he asked, smiling.

"I took it out of Joel's car and made a copy when he wasn't home. My mother didn't raise a complete fool!"

"If no one admits it, it's your word against theirs," he commented offhand. "He'll want to come into court as if he is the injured party. He will tell the judge that you are crazy, you know."

"I certainly hope so! A crazy woman can't possibly take care of herself or ever handle a job."

"Rhonda…"

"Don't worry. I'll impress the judge, and no one will be able to lie unless, of course, they're sitting on their brains."

Sawyer laughed heartily at this. "You intend on playing to win?"

"Now I do," she said firmly. "My husband taught me a great lesson these past few weeks. With a relationship, it's not how you play the game that's important. What counts is if you win or lose. I plan to win. No one remembers the loser, do they?"

Sawyer said nothing, but pushed the papers across for her to read and sign. As she read, a slight grin crossed her thinning face. *He isn't as conservative as* Peter. She couldn't help thinking. *I hope these bimbos and their husbands have healthy checkbooks.*

She lowered her blond head and signed the papers without flinching. Then Sawyer spoke, clearing his throat. "Rhonda, this is what I think we should do. Let me hold these papers." He had picked them up and was waving them in the air. Rhonda thought he looked ridiculous waving his arms, and started to laugh.

He immediately threw them on the desk, smiled broadly and began again. "When we get to court, young lady, I want to win as much above the 50 percent you're guaranteed as possible. I will hold these papers for eighteen months and you call if you want him served at any time. Make copies of everything and put them in a safe place. Get a safety deposit box in your name only, for all-important valuables. He cannot get into it, unless you die, of course. Then who cares anyway? My advice to you is to treat this as a business. He's older than you and hopefully you will outlive him and get it all. You'll be able to live comfortably on what I feel you can get, but I can't guarantee anything. The only guarantee in life is death, unfortunately. Since you're not well, you obviously can't take on a job to supplement your income. Besides, at this time in your life why should you have to reduce your lifestyle? Old Joel is responsible for your bills as long as he's married to you. I say, turn your head, and do as you damn well please. Enjoy yourself for now. But if he files against you, we'll contest it for three years and drag him through the courts. He'll be sixty-three by the time it's over. If he gets nasty, I can file a Protection from Abuse order against him and have him out in twenty-four hours. If he hits you, call the police. Insist on pictures being taken. Go to the women's shelter and call me immediately."

He handed her a card with his beeper number on it, as well as the office number.

"Are you sure he doesn't know you have cancer?" he asked without taking a breath.

Rhonda shook her head.

"Well, tell him. Tell your family! That should really make him feel good about himself. It's your call. What do you say?" For a brief instant Rhonda felt the emotional pain creeping back into her frail body and thought of God's hand extended toward Adam on the ceiling of the Sistine chapel. Touching depicts the gift of life. Joel had touched the very core of her being emotionally and had almost destroyed her. Did he not know that the skin is the human body's largest organ? A simple touch on the hand, an arm around a waist can reduce heart rate and lower blood pressure. *I will tell him about my cancer* she thought, all the while knowing there would be no emotional support to help her through the pain. There would be no touches to stimulate the release of endorphins, the body's natural pain suppressors. She would be on her own in that department.

They shook hands and she told him she would pay his secretary on the way out. As she was writing the check to give to his secretary, Sawyer popped his head out of the door. "Hey, Rhonda," he said with the grin of a school boy trying to make points with his teacher. "Don't worry , everything will turn out fine, we are going to give him a run for his money!

By the way, the 'K' stands for Kendall, my mother's maiden name."

"Why, you read my mind!" Rhonda shouted back, laughing. "What is your birth sign?"

"I'm a fish, he shouted. Why?"

"Never mind. I'll explain it to you when you're older," she laughed. And out the door she went.

The drive home felt refreshing to her in the morning spring air. She pressed the button to let the window finish its fall. The air felt so good on her pale skin, "almost as refreshing as a douche," she said. Then, after a few seconds had passed, she began talking to herself again, "My, Rhonda, what a dirty old lady you've become." She now laughed out loud.

Alone as usual at home, Rhonda started to write a list of the things she needed to pick up at the grocery store. Her thoughts began to drift back to the conversation during the office visit with Sawyer. He doesn't realize that I probably don't have eighteen months, she thought. She immediately sat down and wrote four notes on her personal stationary and then took out a large tablet and quickly wrote a very long letter. She placed everything in a large manila envelope addressed to Sawyer. She then placed the addressed envelope into another larger envelope and addressed it to her trusted friend , Marti. Having completed the tasks at hand she made a quick call to Marti and told her that she would be receiving a large envelope. " When I am gone, please open it and mail the envelope inside." Marti did not question Ronnie about the envelope and they never spoke about it again after this day. Marti would do what was requested without ever questioning why or what for and Ronnie knew this. She could not turn off her thoughts. Life had once been so uncomplicated. Now an ordinary day was just hoping to make it to the next. Joe and Park called often. How delightful it was just to hear their voices. Some lessons can be very cruel. Life certainly is full of peaks and valleys. " What am I supposed to learn?" She now spoke out loud looking toward heaven. "Forgive me for complaining. I know there are many chosen women with larger crosses then mine out there. I also know that many suffer in silence. May I gently remind you Lord, that it was you who bestowed upon me a sharp mind. The sharp tongue, however, I most likely developed on my own. Take this burden from me and grant me peace, Lord. Life has come almost full circle and I am just not strong enough to do all the things that must be done. Please give me the strength to do what is right and enjoy the time I have left. We'll talk again, soon." With that, Rhonda walked to the car. She could not shut out her thoughts.

I just want to smile, get in my car, drive to the mall, charge what I want and never see the bill. After twenty-nine years of hard labor, I deserve it! This pain pill should start working soon and relieve some of my back pain. She swallowed. *I'm so tired.*

As she was driving to the mall, the car radio was playing <u>Strangers in the Night</u>. Instead of changing the station she reached over and turned it off. "I don't want to hear about love anything!" she shouted to no one except herself. "Love is an action. Love is an action," she repeated out loud, taunting herself. "If love's an action, Joel, you only love yourself. By your actions it doesn't take rocket science to know you sure don't love me. When you love someone, you don't screw around when you think no one's watching. Come to think of it, I wonder if you ever did or even know what love is." Her mind was racing now, but the pain was beginning to take charge of her thought processes.

By the time she had reached the mall, she knew her energy level had once again been drained by the pain that now seemed to be her constant companion . . . something that was always there when you didn't want it and guaranteed to give you the hurt of your life. As she pulled in front of Neiman Marcus to park, she spotted her friend, Diedra Kane. Diedra was smiling as always and noticed Rhonda's car when she drove in.

She is still beautiful inside and out, Rhonda thought as Diedra walked over to the car. Rhonda had always loved Diedra, probably because she had accepted Rhonda for who she was and

40

had never been judgmental of anyone's actions. Marti always told Diedra exactly the way things were as did Rhonda. Most importantly, Diedra never tired to change either of them. It was always such a good feeling to have someone accept you for who you are and not want you to be what they think you should be.

Diedra's husband had passed away three years ago. Everyone in the community kept saying that she would be all right. After all, he left her well off. This attitude really hit a nerve with Rhonda. She and Marti had discussed it often.

"If you have money, you are not supposed to bleed or hurt like everyone else in this town," Marti had spoken angrily one particular afternoon. "They all make me sick!"

"Diedra has given to everyone her entire life, and I can't believe the very people she helped are so callous to her pain," Rhonda had said. "They talk about her as if she doesn't have any feelings. But who is the first one there to help them when things go wrong? Her husband was sick for such a long time and I never heard her complain. She took care of him and was happy to be able to do it. She asked for nothing from anyone. Are the people from Newton Falls all small minded and self righteous, or is the disease a national one?"

"It is world wide Ron! No one cares about anything but themselves these days, underline especially in this place. People love it when you're down. It's something to gossip about. I found out a long time ago there is virtually no one, well, maybe a very limited amount of people who are happy if anyone they know gets ahead of them. Even if they think someone is getting ahead of them the remarks start, always trying to make the other person's success seem like sour grapes. No one is happy for anyone else now a days! Success around here breeds contempt!"

"Diedra has something most can never attain, Marti. It's something called class."

"Right! Hey, Ron I'm always right, aren't I?"

Rhonda laughed with her dearest friend and smugly answered, "Right!"

Diedra had now approached the side of the car and was tapping on the window as Rhonda reached for the small bottle of water she kept hidden beneath the seat.

"What's wrong sweetie?" Diedra asked in a very concerned tone. "Every time I see you it seems you're taking a pill. You've got to let me help you! Marti won't discuss you with anyone and when I mention how thin you are she changes the subject. You and I need to talk, girl!"

"Well, actually Diedra, Marti and I have this secret pact to destroy the world and all information is on a need to know basis. If she told you our secrets, we would have to kill you." Hearing this, Diedra laughed, but refused to drop the issue.

"You were there for me when I needed someone. I haven't forgotten! Honestly, I love Marti and your sons but you need more people in your life to help you get through whatever's going on besides Joel's escapades."

"God does work in mysterious ways," Mama had always told Rhonda. "The people that pass through each of our lives are for a purpose. Don't always question, child? Grow with the knowledge you have gained by the experience, whether it be good or bad. Learn to let go and let God! You do not always have to understand the journey. Just try and take something good from it."

Rhonda popped the pill with the help of the bottled water that she now held in her hands, even managing a smile for one of her cherished friends.

"Come on, I'll buy you a cup of hazelnut coffee," Diedra said softly. "Let's talk." Together, they entered the mall and managed to find a corner booth inside the Java Hut.

They both remained silent until coffee was served. Diedra was the first to break it. "What's up Ronnie? Please tell me. Let me help. You and Marti can't carry the world on your shoulders alone. I can be strong too!" With that, Rhonda's eyes welled up into tears. She took a sip of coffee, looked Diedra straight in the eyes and began.

For two hours they sat there together, both oblivious to their surroundings while Rhonda mostly talked with Diedra interrupting only to ask pertinent questions concerning the cancer. Rhonda told her everything about the cancer, the lawyers that she had visited, how the boys were handling everything, and all that she knew so far about Joel's latest escapades. When Rhonda was exhausted, she abruptly stopped with, "That's exactly the way it is, De, and you got it straight from the horse's mouth!"

Now the tears were running down Diedra's beautiful face. She could always feel the pain of others, possibly because she had endured so much during her own life. "I will discuss this with no one ever, accept to tell Marti in private that you and I have discussed this problem."

"Does Joel know?" Diedra quietly asked.

"Right!" Rhonda managed to make a joke out of something serious. "We are going to a hockey game next week, together for a change. I plan to tell him then. Unless he's absolutely crazy, he must realize that for the past two years something has been wrong. The fact is that he has fallen in love again, and can't live without the wonderful creature he has found."

"He most likely thinks you just don't love him. You know men! I'll bet he thinks your main problem is the thought of him leaving you. Miss Barracuda has him believing he's the most wonderful person in the world."

"Yeah," Rhonda joked. "The next best thing to money and sliced bread and his retirement plan. I would love to be around in two or three years and let her tell me just how wonderful their life is together. Whom do you think will get caught cheating first, De? Him or her? I'll bet she is cheating on him just like he is her already!"

"She will!" Diedra took a sip of her coffee and spoke with authority. "Look at the track record sweetie. How many men has she had before him? How many women has he fooled around with? At his age I'd say the smart money's on her, but since they are building this trusting relationship on lies and betrayal, it could go either way. It's really not a matter of if or who, but when."

Diedra took a long look at her friend, seeing the exhaustion creeping over her. "What do you say? Are you up to going to Neiman Marcus and treating yourself to something expensive today? Let's go look at diamonds. They don't leave you in the night."

"Neither does jock itch!" Rhonda quickly answered. "Well, De, you now can consider me among the insane ones because right now I care more about chocolate than diamonds." Diedra knew by the sound of her voice and the effort it took her to stand that it was going to be a very short shopping spree. "Do you think there are malls in hell, De?" Rhonda asked as they slowly approached the entrance of the store. Diedra looked over at Rhonda's tiny face and smiled.

Almost inaudibly she said, "You mean this isn't hell?"

Rhonda laughed. "Come on Diedra. You know what ? I could ride in my car to the ends of the earth most days. For some reason it is very soothing for me. But I wouldn't get far without Lady Godiva by my side. That naked chocolate just drives me crazy! I have a need! A need for Godiva chocolate-covered caramels! First stop is the candy counter!"

There was no one on earth that Diedra knew of that could actually make Godiva dark chocolate-covered caramels sound so alluring and sexy, and at the same time illegal, yet so wonderful that you couldn't possibly expect to survive the day without some. No one, that is, except for Rhonda. She, somehow, always managed to see things differently than anyone else.

"I wonder if Joel's little virgin queen has a need for Godiva chocolates?"

"I doubt that, Ron, her needs lie elsewhere. I would say possibly somewhere between Beauty Rest or Simmons." " Good thought, De. You certainly are quick today!"

Chapter Four

Wow, Rhonda thought. *Today is Thursday and this week has just flown by. I've got so many things to take care of this week, and I still have to get my blood test tomorrow.* She already suspected that the blood tumor markers were up and subconsciously was not expecting a good report. The doctors had explained that if the markers were increasing that was an indicator the disease was progressing.

Today, she was going to transfer all the Joel and Rhonda savings accounts to Rhonda accounts. When she arrived at the bank, it was 10:30 A.M., and she had made a mental note to call Angie, the telephone company, and Chris. The pain was getting worse again. She fumbled in her purse for a Darvocette as she stood in line, found two, and placed them in her mouth as though they were Life Savers. *They really are Life-Savers to* me. She mentally chided herself.

When it was her turn in line, she walked up to the teller cage and pulled out the books, laying them firmly in front of her.

"What can I do for you today, Rhonda?" Karen, the teller, asked her.

Rhonda hesitated for a second, then pushed the books forward. "I want to close out these accounts. No! Leave one-hundred dollars in each one."

She and Joel had been going to the same bank for twenty-nine years. The same friendly tellers were still there. *In a small town, changes take place slowly or not at all,* she thought to herself. *Tomorrow, everyone will know.*

"Sure thing," Karen said. "You and Joel leaving the country or something?"

"Sure we are, at 2:00 P.M., in fact!" Rhonda joked back. "Oh, by the way, I want half in a check and the other half in cash, Karen, please."

"No problem Rhonda. How are Park and Joe doing? We haven't seen them for a while." It seems like a month or two since either has been in, unless I've been busy and just didn't see them. Karen spoke nonchalantly as she tallied the interest.

"They're fine," Rhonda lied. "I'll tell them you asked about them."

"How you been feeling? You sure are looking pale lately, you on some liquid diet or what? We can't believe how thin you are any more."

"One can't be too rich or too thin, Karen!" Rhonda joked. *I'm still here, at least for now,* Rhonda silently told herself as she smiled at Karen, who just smiled at Rhonda's remark. Karen had graduated with Joel and always had been very friendly with Rhonda. Karen and Joel had even dated before Rhonda came along. She had always remained very cordial with both of them.

When the transactions were completed, Rhonda told Karen goodbye and left the bank. She then drove to the next town, only five minutes away, and walked into a competing bank that Joel never seemed to think much of for one reason or another. He didn't like the tellers. The bank president, according to Joel, was a cheap son of a bitch. Joel had always told Rhonda that Mr. Arienhart, president of the bank, was nothing but a sneaky little weasel and he had no use for him. She never knew what had transpired between the two of them. Sometimes Joel just took a strange dislike to certain people. She had never pursued the issue.

"Hi," she said as she approached the teller cage. "My name is Rhonda Smith, and I want to open a savings account." She deposited the check and added Joe and Park's names along with her own.

The teller's name was Tammy. She smiled and was seemingly very efficient but lacked a certain personality that the tellers at the other bank seemed to have. After taking the information required, she handed Rhonda the deposit card to sign. Rhonda deposited the check only into the savings account and inquired about renting two safety deposit boxes. Tammy stated that they were certainly available immediately, so Rhonda promptly rented and paid ahead for one year on both boxes out of the cash in her purse. On the first safety deposit box, she put her son's names as well as her own. The second box was in her name solely.

When she was alone in the booth, she promptly put the cash in the box which had three signatures on it. In the box that was solely hers, she placed copies of all Joel's assets. Only he could get in the box if and when she died. Satisfied, she placed the boxes back in the vault and drove home.

While driving, Rhonda's thoughts went back in time to an evening when they had been discussing Joel's friend, Paul Andrews. Paul had been caught cheating and Alice, his wife, was suing for a divorce. " One day you will probably turn into a sneaky jerk too, she had joked."

"Don't be crazy, Ron. You're the best thing that's ever happened to me."

"Well if it happens, I hope you tell me first. I sure wouldn't want to find out from someone else like poor Alice did." " I don't think you have to worry." The sound of the words rang in her mind. She spoke aloud as she turned into her driveway. "Lord, please help me not to look back on yesterday. It hurts too much, and I don't want to lose today or tomorrow."

When she finally pulled into the garage, Rhonda looked into the rear view mirror. "Get a life bitch!" she screamed at the face in the mirror. "He's not worth it!"

She finally got out of the car and slammed its door closed. Slowly, she entered the empty house.

She knew she was getting weaker. The pain killers were needed on a regular basis and sometimes more often. "I must find the strength. Please God, it's you and me now. You've got to help me through this."

The drive home was just enough to help her gather her second wind. She had decided to start collecting evidence for her day in court. First things first. The easiest evidence to get hold of was all of the phone calls coming in and going out of the house. Attorney Sawyer had reminded her. She flung her purse on the chair, picked up the phone and dialed for a service rep. She was immediately taken in the order the call came in. Waiting seemed like an eternity. We all know the routine. Finally, someone named Martha came on line. "Phone number, please," Martha requested.

Rhonda gave the number and the area code.

"One moment, please." This was followed by a few seconds of silence. "Yes, Mrs. Smith, how can we be of service to you?"

Rhonda simply stated that she wanted a printout of every call in and out made from this number for the last six months and for the next six months. "All calls," she told Martha. "Local and long distance."

"There will be a charge, Mrs. Smith," Martha said.

"That's fine," Rhonda stated flatly. "Tell me the amount due and I will get a check off to you today."

"I will need the four digit code on your phone bill just to make sure I'm talking to an authorized person."

Rhonda frantically searched for a copy of the phone bill in a pile of bills on top of the desk. Finally she spotted it. With trembling hands she picked it up and read the four digit code to the service representative.

When she hung up the phone, she promptly made out the check to the telephone company and put it in an envelope to mail. She always picked up the mail from the box and sorted it, so she knew who would get the printouts.

Exhausted, she walked into the small powder room, closed the door, and cried. It seemed she did this so often. "When does the hurt go away?" she wondered aloud. "Why is my life such a mess? What have I done to deserve this?"

As usual, there was no answer. Sickness and the thought of death, be it the death of a marriage or your own life, somehow, has a way of taking us to view the darkest corners of life including our souls. It is not an easy task to live in this darkest of holes. No one should ever have to face it alone. In reality most of us are forced to find our own way. There does seem to be a connection between the nervous system and the immune system that can be triggered by stress. This pathway can leave individuals vulnerable to diseases and even sudden death. Women often keep pursuing the reasons why. During these painful times you really find out who you are. There are no perfect wives or perfect husbands. Unfortunately good wives don't always come with thin thighs, beautiful long hair and a plate of chocolate chip cookies, ready to drop everything and make love as soon as Mr. Wonderful approaches the doorstep.

Didn't it amaze you when a group of Danish researchers announced men have an average of four billion more brain cells apiece than women? If this fact is true, why then in a survey taken by American Woman did 72 % say they would rather win $ 10,000 rather than have one year of really satisfying sex? Obviously the extra brain cells must be inactive. This leads me to believe that after the romance and excitement are gone, the sex must indeed be very boring for most women. What a shame!

Is the answer to accept adultery as the norm? Everyone has times when they feel lonely and unloved in a marriage. There's got to be more than this. Some people are so insecure. They actually set out to find Mr. Perfect. It doesn't matter if he is married or not. It is like buying a new pair of shoes, someone recently told me. " You go in and try on as many as you want to. When you find a pair that is comfortable you take them. Everyone knows at some point the shoes just get old. When that happens you try on a few more new ones and pick out something different." What about love? Love just doesn't happen! It takes a lot of work by both parties. Every and any whore involved with a married man fears that the wife will be able to relight the flame of passion in her husband, and he'll try and go back to her. Short term pleasure always results in long-term pain for all involved. Even the ones involved without any choice in the matter that are receiving no pleasure feel shame, humiliation, hurt, and yes, even guilt! Most men cheat because they really believe they can get away with it. The wife should spell out the rules for him in very plain English. Once the rules are redefined, if he cheats get rid of him. At this point, I think, it is safe to say they deserve each other. Her commitment has the same value as his. **ZERO!!** The wife has lost nothing but a loser! If any woman is running around with a married man, she has to have left her brains on another planet. How can she possibly believe that any commitment he gives her is worth anything when he obviously doesn't keep the ones that are supposed to be most important ones in life. The rules are the same for cheating wives.

Never forget the Dorothy Hutelmyer case! The jury awarded Dorothy Hutelmyer $500,000 for alienation of affection, which means her husband's new wife stole her husbands love and another $500,000 for criminal conversation, which means that he and his new love committed adultery. In some states you cannot sue for alienation of affection but you are able to get around this by suing for indignities, which can be more profitable in the long run.

With the new season, the weather started to change and each day seemed warmer. Lately, Rhonda had been taking long walks in the cemetery. It was so peaceful there, "Why not get used to the place," she told herself. "Not one person there can hurt me," she had told Marti during one of their many conversations. Marti called sometimes two or three times a day just to check on Rhonda because she sensed Rhonda was thinking about suicide once again. And she was right.

"Once in awhile, life can be more painful than death seems to be," Rhonda had told her not so long ago.

Marti also knew that Rhonda carried a revolver for protection and so every time she heard the sound of an ambulance, Rhonda's phone would ring. Marti's cheerful voice would always be on when Rhonda picked up. "Hi, Rhonda. What are you up to today?" It was her subtle way to check, and they both knew it.

"I want a divorce," she had told Marti. " I just can't live with someone that doesn't really love me. I am numb. It's very scary to feel nothing. Can you actually love someone that hates you, and you can not trust? Maybe I am as stupid and ugly as he tells me I am."

"Stay there. Don't you dare leave! You need hospitalization and you have a roof over your head. Besides that, you can't go to work. You know what the doctor said? Even if you think you can work, as sick as you get, who will put up with it?" Marti had been there plenty of mornings. She would stop on her way to work to check on Rhonda. Often the entire hour would pass with Rhonda in the bathroom throwing up and then retching with dry heaves until all her energy was spent. Marti would practically carry her to bed before she left for work. On these days she would pray that Rhonda would just sleep and not try and get up. The boys were good to call and check on her at least. Joel seldom ever called unless it was to leave a message that he would not be home for one reason or another. If by chance he would come in ,he never bothered to check on her.

"I know for certain that Joel certainly doesn't knock you around. You have everything except love and emotional support. God loves you and you have lots of friends and a family that cares what happens to you! The boys need you! You are the only stable factor in their life at the moment."

"How can someone share their dreams with one woman and give his love to another?" Rhonda asked, not really listening. "This emotional stress has killed part of me, Marti, and the cancer is taking care of the rest."

Thinking back was something Rhonda had great difficulty with. It was painful, but she couldn't seem to shut off her brain. Thoughts of conversations with friends, especially Marti, and thoughts about Joel and the pain she saw in her sons' eyes all haunted her. *I dub myself the Queen of Rejection*, she had thought while bathing the previous day. And to make it official, she picked up the shampoo bottle and dumped the contents on her blond hair.

At that point, she started laughing out loud as her thoughts traveled back to the evening prior. She had gotten so angry with Joel when he told her she didn't need him anyway. He just couldn't close the door on Cassie. She really needed him. Rhonda was hurt. The war of words had begun again.

"You put that whore before me, Joel? How dare you?!" she had screamed. "Well, let me tell you something, Mr. King of the Ass-holes in love with a whore! That thing between your legs won't work forever and she'll be running on you. But this," and she lifted one leg of her frail body higher than even she thought possible, "will last forever," she screamed, pointing to her vagina with her free hand.

"Garbage!" he shouted back at her. "That's what you are, and so is that! Garbage!"

"You liked this garbage for a lot of years, Dickhead! You're screwing real garbage now, so I guess that makes you the Garbage Man! That's what you've become! Trash attracts trash! You are already dead... just too stupid to know it. She has reduced you to dirt. You are exactly like her... filthy dirt!"

"No one gets the total package!" He screamed as he paced, not knowing what was coming next.

"You had it you fool! You just chose to trade it in for something that has been passed around both counties. She is the total package all right! Used by all!" Rhonda slammed the door is his face, shutting him out. His eyes had looked like two cesspools of fire! She no longer recognized the person he had become.

She rinsed her hair and toweled herself off, stepping out of the bathtub. "I'm married to the King of Ass-holes with two nick names, hence forth to be called Dickhead or Garbage Man," she laughingly taunted to no one out loud. And to make it official she reached for a bottle of Joel's favorite cologne on the closet shelf. Calmly, she emptied over half of the cologne in the commode and proceeded to fill the balance of the bottle with her urine. Silently, she capped the cologne bottle, washed, quickly rinsed and dried it off, replacing it on the shelf where it was.

"There, lover," she said to no one, "your title is now official!" *Now I know where the term 'Piss on you!' came from*, she thought, seemingly pleased with her newfound knowledge.

When couples have reached this point in a marriage, I have found that the words are always the same. How quickly we learn and use the vulgar street language is truly amazing. Hurt is no respecter of race, religion, education, or background. The hateful words always surface quickly and so easily reduce each of us to the animals that all through life we proclaimed we were above being reduced to! We are reacting to an action, not making a choice. I remember, Father Bill once told me to love my enemies and pray for them. "When someone is mean and hateful, it is hard to turn the other cheek. That person needs your love. God is ever faithful in his promises. Make the choice to respond in love. God's word promises it will be the same as if you have dumped hot burning coals on their head." Rhonda often thought of that one conversation with the priest, a gentle man of God.

She dressed as quickly as she could. It was late when she finished but she had made a very important luncheon engagement a month ago and she intended to keep it.

Since childhood, or as far back as she could remember, she had to know things and always had to find out for herself. Mama knew how she was. Some things just never change. "Rhonda," she used to say when she was a teenager, "you should take a few minutes and read the Bible. Now she encouraged her to read Ecclesiastes, Chapter One, Verse Eighteen[7]. Sometimes things are easier to handle if left alone. It's not fun to be one of God's chosen women[8]. You will only increase your sadness!"

"I deal better with honesty and truth, Mama," she had said that afternoon so many years ago. Rhonda had always run her life on that premise and was driven by something even she could not explain. Lying had always made her crazy. Her father had always been the same way so she just figured it was an inherent trait. She had always vowed to herself that she would never marry someone that lied to her. When a boyfriend lied to her once as a teenager about something as small and stupid as his grade point average, she never went out with him again. Everyone has something quirky in their personality and this just happened to be part of Rhonda's make-up.

"Why sneak and lie?" she had asked Joel. "For God's sake, a real man should be honest and have enough integrity to tell his wife the truth, even if it hurts. Make the playing field fair! Besides, I deserve to know who. You owe me that! After all, I've slept with everyone you've slept with and everyone your whores have slept with. I'm sure if they shack up with you, they've shacked up with many men before you ever came along. How stupid are you? Have you become a complete fool? If she's doing you, she'll do it again with someone else. It's not a matter of 'if' but 'when.' You don't have a private lock on her body! Or have you invested some of our money in chastity belts for your conquests? I'm not responsible for your choices; that's your problem! I want you to know that everything in life comes with a price, and I truly hope you can afford to cash the checks you have written. I'm going to make choices also. Since you

---

[7] For in much wisdom is much grief: and he that increaseth knowledge increaseth sorrow.

[8] Women who's husbands cheat and they know it.

refuse to talk to me about the direction you have chosen, my alternatives are limited." There! She had stated her case.

"Why don't you just die?!" Joel shouted back in anger, still refusing to address the real issue. "You want to make something dirty out of something beautiful!"

"Something, Joel? Why not call it what it is? It's called intercourse, you ass-hole or do you know it by another name? It's all the same! You can call it by any name you choose but it's still exactly what you think I have reduced it to.. My husband has sex on demand with someone else's wife and thinks it is the best he can get! Sounds really beautiful to me…Yep…Beautiful…Dam right Beautiful…In fact it's about the most beautiful thing I've ever heard!" Rhonda was bordering on the brink of hysteria. Joel looked ready to kill. His muscles were twitching and his dark eyes gleamed like two cess pools from hell. He had a look of uncontrollable rage on his face, yet Rhonda was not willing to back down. Strangely enough she did not fear him. She had already dealt with her own mortality and at this moment was not fearful of death. "It's not beautiful at all! Why doesn't the whore expend the energy on her own marriage instead of you? Think about it!" Who is getting seconds, you or her husband?"Do you really think he has taken the vow of celibacy?

"If you get hurt, that's your problem! I plan to do whatever makes me feel good! So get used to it! You know what your problem is? You're afraid of being left alone. No one wants you, Rhonda. You're old! You're angry because someone younger than you wants me and she thinks I'm wonderful. It's eating you alive because you don't think so. You are the typical pathetic, aging female who is no longer able to compete!"

"Well Dickhead, because of your dirty, yes dirty, escapades, I tested positive for HPV. Do you know what that is? How can you stand there and tell me how wonderful it is? I'm the only one paying for it. You and your whore are coming out totally unscathed and I hate both of you. I could kill both of you and never look back!" She screamed with the look of murder flashing in her raging blue eyes.

Joel quickly grabbed her purse from the chair, took out the loaded revolver and shoved it into her hands. "Go ahead and shoot me!" he screamed with uncontrollable rage. "Anything is better than living with you, even death!"

Rhonda looked at the loaded revolver she now held firmly. She pointed it directly at Joel. She glanced down at the revolver, then looked Joel straight in the eyes. Joel stood there, not flinching an iota, anticipating her next move.

She slowly lowered the revolver and placed it on a nearby table. Joel's face did not even show a hint of relief and he still had not moved. She realized he hated anyone he felt challenged by, especially if in his mind he felt they were mentally stronger.

Rhonda now added to the tension growing between them, speaking in a calm and normal tone of voice, knowing exactly which buttons to push. "Your problem is that you had it all and threw it away for a strange piece of well used ass, just like Paul Andrews! You have been so busy with your conquests over the years. You were too stupid to really find out who I am. I didn't shoot you, not because I love you. Love has nothing to do with it. I didn't shoot you because you're not worth it! I'm smarter than you, Cassie, Jan and Cindy combined and I feel nothing for you except pity. Your so-called friends laugh behind your back and massage your ego to your face. When you sleep with the sergeant you get no respect from the troops! Doesn't Cassie even know that much? Oh, yeah, I forgot her brain was dislocated. I don't have to tell you where to find it. I'm sure you have had contact with it more than I care to know."

"There are worse things than being a whore," he retorted.

"You are right about that, Joel," she quickly responded. "What's worse than being a whoremaster without any integrity? Integrity is what you do when no one can see what you're doing and no one else but you knows and yet you still do the honest and right thing, in case you have forgotten. She has even robbed you of that and you don't even know it!" Rhonda had now raised her voice to a level just below screaming.

"Fuck you, Rhonda!" Joel screamed louder now, matching her.

Rhonda was getting frustrated. After all, she knew Joel better than he knew himself. It seemed so important for her to have the last word, especially now. "You already have, 'Garbage Man,' but you'll never in this lifetime touch me again!"

"Is that a threat?"

"At this, Rhonda literally lost it and started laughing, more at the child that seemed more prevalent in him than at the man.

"No, Joel," she said smiling broadly, trying to contain herself. "That's a fact! You can take it to the bank."

Joel turned around slowly and didn't say another word. He walked into the den and put on a CD. As Rhonda walked up the stairs, she could hear the music play. He had put on Reba McIntyre and was playing one of her songs that goes "Does he love you like he loves me? Does he think of you when he's holden' me? Does he whisper all his fantasies? Does he love you like he's been lovin' me?"[9]

Totally exhausted, she fell across the bed and went to sleep, but this time there were no tears. Joel knew, and so did she, there were no get-out-of-jail-free cards left for her to give him. Once, she had loved him more than anything in the world. He had at last managed to kill every emotion and feeling she had ever held close to her heart. He had hurt her and wounded her more than anything or anyone ever could in this world! Why did God say that she had to forgive?

"As she fell asleep, her thoughts drifted to a passage written by George Roemisch:

Forgiveness is the fragrance of the violet which still clings fast to the heel that crushed it. Forgiveness is the broken dream which hides itself within the corner of the mind oft called forgetfulness so that it will not bring pain to the dreamer.

---

[9] Does he love you like he loves me? Artist Reba McIntyre

Chapter Five

Rhonda looked at her watch. She was nearly ready to go but was surprised that the time was 1:15. It was only a five minute trip to the restaurant and she didn't want to make a grand entrance. Everyone she had bumped into lately seemed to find a way to make a remark about Joel, always managing to make a back handed comment about her physical appearance or what she should do, such as I'd get rid of him if I were you, or you don't deserve this, or wow you look bad! You've gotten so thin! Get rid of him. She really didn't want to face anyone else and have to be polite and listen to their advice. If everyone in the area knew for such a long time, she wondered why no one had thought enough of her to come and tell her. Now everyone she met was full of advice. If C.J. was running true to form, he would be late anyway.

C.J. and Rhonda had grown up together and he had always adored her. They had kept in touch throughout the years. He had always hovered over her like an older brother would with a younger sister. She still remembered when they were both in the first grade. First and second grade were in the same room. On the second school day he had cleaned Jamie Robertson's clock because he had pulled Rhonda's pigtails and made her cry. They had taken turns carrying each others books home even up through high school, written brief notes to each other during college and discussed relationships openly with each other. C.J. had remained the one constant in her life. *How lucky I am*, she thought to herself while making the short jaunt to the Julious Restaurant. *C.J. is still my friend and it's been fifty years. Where has all the time gone to?*

C.J. was married again for the third time. She recalled one of the notes he had written. The messages were always similar: *Guess what? I've found a new love. She's wonderful! You'll love her. Love and kisses, C.J.*

"Third times a charm," he had told Rhonda. She had hoped so, because his first two wives had cheated on him and it had almost destroyed the big easy-going guy Rhoda admired. He was kind, always managing to find the time to do nice things for everyone, loved the whole world, somehow always played it straight. Rhonda often wondered why he always had to deal with so much personal emotional pain himself.

"I'd be delighted to meet you for lunch. Heck, I'll even buy!" he had joked on the phone. "How 'bout I bring my new love so you can meet her?"

"Not this time. This time, I want it to be just you and me. I need to talk."

"No problem kid," C.J. was always so up. "You want to meet me outside or inside?"

"Inside."

"OK! See you soon!" C.J. said and hung up the phone.

"What a shame!" Rhonda said to herself as she drove into the parking lot of the restaurant. "His first two wives have no idea of what they lost!" Again she spoke out loud to no one but herself.

Rhonda recalled the years when she and C.J. were in college. C.J. had written one of his famous memos to Rhonda. He had heard an interview given by Ricardo Montalban. Mr. Montalban was asked the question of what he thought love was. He thought for only a second and then replied. "A great lover is someone who can satisfy one woman her entire lifetime and be satisfied with that one woman his entire lifetime. It is not someone who goes from woman to woman; any dog can do that!"

Rhonda was smiling as she turned off the ignition of the car. When C.J. had written that note to her, it had ended with *I guess someone out there knows who I really am! Call me soon! ~C.J.* She had returned the call and chided him about the note. "You are going to get your heart broken a million times, C.J. Everything in life cannot be taken at face value. The women that you always fall in love with seem to have another agenda in mind. Be careful who you love!"

She exited the car and walked toward the Julious Restaurant, still in her own world. A large pleasant man came up behind her and lightly tugged at the curls on the back of her head.

Rhonda squealed delightfully as she turned around to greet the stranger, knowing just who it was. "C.J.!"

"I'd know those legs anywhere!" he said laughing and hugging her at the same time.

For a fleeting moment, Rhonda did not have that empty feeling deep inside that had been her constant companion for so long. "The human touch is such a wonderful gift! People should hug more." With that they strolled arm and arm into the familiar old restaurant. It felt like old times again.

Jimmy, the restaurant's aging cook, yelled as C.J. and Rhonda entered the restaurant. "Annie we got us trouble here."

It seemed like old times. Here they were at the Julious Restaurant. Jimmy and Annie Catera had opened the restaurant more than forty years ago and Marti, one of Rhonda's dearest friends, was their daughter. Old Jim had always loved Spanish names so Annie had indulged him when they named the restaurant. It hadn't hurt business any. People for miles around ate there and raved about Annie's cooking through the years. Everyone went there! The menu was still the same, (good old-time Italian food) plentiful and delicious. Even the smell could make you hungry for everything on the menu.

Annie came quickly from the kitchen looking all flustered. When she looked up and saw C.J. she smiled broadly and hollered. "C.J.! And look here will you Jimmy? It's Rhonda! The only one missing is our Marti. It seems almost like old times. I'll fix you something special, Rhonda, sweetie, you need some fat on those bones! Is my Marti coming too?" Annie talked a mile a minute, running everything together without even taking a breath.

"No Annie, she's got a full schedule today. We talked on the phone late last night though."

As C.J. and Annie talked, Rhonda's mind drifted. C.J. had proclaimed his love at five for her the day they entered the first grade. Who would ever believe fifty two years, three wives and four children that he would be delighted to meet her for lunch.

"How ya doin, kid?" He asked while joking on the phone. "How's old Joel getting along? That old dog. Can he still get it up?" She only laughed and ignored the questions.

When Marti, C.J. and Rhonda were children, they had spent many of their childhood days getting in Annie's way in the kitchen. Annie had always given them a small chore, like drying the silverware or folding napkins, so they would feel useful. But most of the time was spent laughing talking and eating. Annie had grown to love Rhonda and C.J. as if they were her own and the feelings were mutual.

When the talking and hugging ended, C.J. and Ronnie took the same familiar table they always sat at while they were growing up.

C.J. helped Ronnie get seated. "God Ronnie, I must really be getting old. For some reason I never realized how tiny you are!"

"Stop it C.J.!" Ronnie laughed. "To a big brother you always remain the smaller one, no matter how old and fat you get!"

"What is the honor of this luncheon?" C.J. flashed that old familiar smile. "It's not every day I can have a lunch with the girl of my childhood dreams."

Just then Annie interrupted, bringing coffee, salad and her famous hot rolls. "Just to start with Ronnie. Jimmy is starting the beef medallions for me and I'll bring you a side dish of cheese sticks and some penne pasta with garlic and oil, your favorite!"

Rhonda thanked Annie lovingly. "You never forget! How do you do it?"

Annie smiled to herself as an answer came to mind. "How can someone forget when they love someone?"

C.J. and Rhonda both picked up a fork, speared a roll and simultaneously reached for the large bowl of salad. They both laughed, filling the restaurant with warmth. C.J. tried to talk as he stuffed salad greedily into his mouth. "It's not the salad; it's that damn special dressing she makes."

"I know! I remember when we were in high school and you tried to talk Marti into stealing it so we could get it made and get rich!" They both laughed in unison.

"Annie never wrote it down! You remember when Marti questioned her about? She got angrier than an old wet hen. We could have made big bucks, Ron!" C.J. said as a matter of fact.

"Sure C.J. Another one of your infamous get rich quick schemes. I really don't think we want to go there, do you?" Rhonda laughed at the thought of it all.

"Annie brought the cheese sticks, beef medallions and penne pasta while they were still eating the salads, teasing. "You kids eat up. Don't make me feel bad now! I can't sit and chat today, we have a big dinner party tonight for fifty people and Jimmy still worries I won't have everything ready! Men!" She laughed before turning to leave them alone.

"By all means, please leave the check!" Rhonda called before Annie could escape into the kitchen. "C.J. is treating today."

"No check, Jimmy and I still aren't too old to take care of our own. Enjoy. It's our treat!"

"Thanks Annie," they both chanted together with C.J. adding, I can't really afford to feed two women anyway!" Annie lumbered to the kitchen throwing up her arms as he spoke.

It was obvious that age was taking its toll, but she and Jimmy refused to retire or sell. Marti had begged them to no avail and had finally just given up. "When God wants them, he'll take care of it," she had told Ronnie. "At least I know in my heart that they'll both go to heaven, not like us Ron. We are both so calculating. Hell is a certainty!"

"Remember when our mothers told us the past was important because it makes us who we are?" Rhonda had answered.

Marti quickly shot back a response. "How could I ever forget? You had C. J. and me thinking that they meant we were all going to die soon. We went to confession every day! Remember, that priest told us if we tried to confess our sins from the past one more time he'd skin us alive."

"Yeah, I remember. That's when I knew we would all go to hell for sure. He must have thought we were real nut cases, after all, how many sins from the past does a ten-year-old kid have? But I also remember you telling me not to worry about hell because hell was just like the mall. You had overheard your dad telling that to your mom. We all knew Jimmy wouldn't lie."

"Do you think there are malls in hell?"

"I really do hope so!" Marti answered that day as they parted company and they both had laughed.

For a few seconds she and C.J. had been quietly eating. He was patiently waiting for her to tell him what was on her mind. Finally, he broke the silence and pulled Rhonda from her thoughts. "What's wrong? You're never this quiet unless something is really bothering you. That I know for sure! The only time in your life that you were quiet was when we were ten and you had us all convinced that we were going to die and go to hell!"

"How can you know me when I don't even know me?"

"Some things never change," C.J. retorted.

"I'm going to tell you. But please don't interrupt me because I may not be able to finish, if you do. I don't want your sympathy but I desperately need your help."

"You've got it."

She taunted him with a coy look. "You're right. Some things just never change. Do you want the shock now or when you're finished eating?"

"Now Ron!" he shot back at her. "Give."

After a long silent pause, she finally began. "It's like this. Joel has been cheating on me for thirty-some odd years and I'm sick of it. Now it's worse than ever. He flaunts his women everywhere. The whole town knows, everyone where he works knows and… worst of all, my sons know. He is not the same person, in fact, he has become more like a dog in heat chasing around with Cassie Porter, Jan Kendal, and Cindy Pressman plus I don't know who else. There have been many others before any of these came along. He thought Jan was hot shit. Sent her over drinks, the entire routine . . . you know how that goes. Jan really fell for his bull and started to get serious so he kinda dumped her for a more accessible piece, Cassie. She worked for him. More under him I should say; however, when Cassie couldn't make it, old Cindy was always there . . . hell, she always has been for thirty years. Even when her first old man was around she made on bones about being available to Joel. Yet, he still nails Jan if he can sneak away once in awhile!

After he humiliated the boys and me with Cassie, openly admitting it, I was done. I just do not want to deal with this kind of thing any more. I am tired, old, and sick. I want to enjoy my life for the time I have left. I want quality and true happiness. Cassie is pulling him around by his ho- ho and he is more than willing to eliminate both his sons and me from his life. Problem is I need concrete evidence for court because I want to charge everyone with indignities and I intend to win. In addition, I need more than 50 percent to survive on. I have no plans to change my current life style and want to be able to leave Joe and Park at least part of what is rightfully theirs because I'm certain that whatever bimbo Joel winds up with will want to make sure her brats or she alone will get whatever she thinks they've got coming to them. Joe and Park won't see a dime after I'm gone.

And now for the surprise of your life . . . I have cancer and I have to win. I haven't done anything before because it never reached these proportions and I needed the hospitalization. I will be haunted by the hurt Joe and Park had to go through as long as I live. I should have left years ago but felt the boys shouldn't have to suffer because of my choices. At least, he tried to be a good father. He is just waiting for me to die. The boys were hurt more deeply than I imagined possible and are so ashamed of him. They are polite to his face but don't want to be seen with him, try not to even be around anyone that knows him. They adored him so and used to be so proud that he was their father. Now, that they know what he is and what he does when he isn't home, they have lost all respect and trust for him. The really sad part about it all is Joel doesn't even realize it. He is caught up to the max in his own secret world. Everyone knows about his dirty little escapades and yet he still puts on this big front for the public and the people that work for him. He has himself believing that everyone is his friend. Any one of them, including the women, would sell him down the drain in less than a minute flat! He is going to fight me for everything we have. Poor Cassie needs him and they have so much in common he refuses to close the door on her. So he thinks. He believes anything she tells him. She would never lie ,of course! Lying to her husband and children doesn't count. She would never lie to Joel. He's literally nuts! Anyway, that's it in a nutshell."

Her eyes filled with tears. C.J. had stopped eating. His dark flashing eyes looked as if he were going to go into a rage and explode. His face was turning red and it was very evident he was trying to squelch the inner rage that he was feeling.

He took a big sip of coffee and yelled for Gino the Bartender to bring him a double. The old bartender brought the drink to C.J. and he promptly ordered another.

"That will serve no purpose C.J." Rhonda could hardly get the words out now, trying to choke back the tears.

"Are you sure, Ron?" C.J. asked quietly. "You've got to be certain! There is no room for mistakes!"

"Because the facts are always ignored doesn't mean they actually no longer exist."

"I called the phone company, so I'll get a printout of all phone calls in and out from both car phones and the home phones. His pals call me after golf and tell me where I can find him. Angie calls me and so does everyone else he works with. Everyone calls to tell me what he's doing, who he's doing it with, and where they're doing it. Do you believe that all these people have my best interest at heart? Even the women are brazen enough to call and ask if he's home. When I ask if there's a message it's always the same. 'Oh, no message. I know where I can find him then.' Hell, I'm glad they have some idea where he is. The boys and I can only reach him by beeper.

They all call my sons and go into explicit detail about meeting him in the afternoon, at McDonald's, the motels or after aerobics class. They have told the boys unthinkable things that they and Joel do together. Each has called and even given me updates. But he won't believe it.

You know what he told me last week? 'Cassie is not a threat to you. She would never do anything to hurt you.' What should I do C.J.? Hold a telethon for him? Does he think sleeping around doesn't hurt me? I hope one day someone cuts his heart out! Hopefully it will hurt so badly that it will dawn on him what the pain is I feel! 'Get over it' everyone says. I'll get over it and get even at the same time in my own way. I have made a promise to God when it's all over I will not waste my time hating him or the women or woman that he has chosen over me. I will pray for them because it will help me to heal according to Father Bill. In my heart I know the feelings I will have are only pity and sorrow for them. In the meantime, let the games begin!

He's has killed me emotionally. It was not a crime of passion or even a rage. He just systematically went about life destroying me, a little bit at a time. With each new conquest of his, I died inside a little more. In my own mind it was a choice Joel made without even a thought of his family or me as far as I'm concerned. Is he really that stupid C.J.? The whore sleeps with my husband but still can't face me. If anyone puts steak in front of Joel, he'll eat it. It never bothered him if the steak belonged to someone else! She rattled on. What the hell does he think hurts me? Her statements, I know he only repeated. 'Let me help you honey I wouldn't hurt you, I just want to sleep your husband!' What about her husband and her poor children? Has everyone forgotten what it is to be faithful?" Suddenly, Rhonda stopped talking, realizing she was rambling on.

C.J. finally took a deep breath and downed a fresh drink. "I've been there, Ron! Some men and women are so depraved. They can justify just about anything. It's easier to find someone else for sex than work on what they have at home. People can make themselves discontent with anything in life. I've had two wives which will prove that out. I could never give them enough. No matter what it was they always wanted more. More money, more sex, more jewelry, newer house, newer car. More, more, more! These types of people are never contented with what the good Lord gave them. The ones with no backbone just find someone else with a little more money and move on. They are willing to do whatever it takes to climb up the social economic ladder . Each year they are older and more frightened and willing to do more to attain the goal. These women want someone to love and appreciate them and are looking for emotional support. In the end, I really wonder how many end up alone, the biggest fear of all. They're so stupid to choose married men. If they'd use their brain instead of their... you know what, they'd know they can boost any guy's ego and get him. There are lots of single, well heeled guys around. They should know if a married man is that easy they'll end up getting nothing, just like he gives his wife. Seventy percent of married women are having affairs and fifty-four percent of their husbands don't even know it. Is everyone in this world insecure or just looking for something they think they can't get or are to lazy to work on at home. It sure is a great world we are leaving for our kids. Pretty soon without a D.N.A. test you won't be able to get married! Hell, I think everyone should get the tests before hand and keep them on file. That way you would at least know if you were related. It's getting scary out there!"

"Well, everyone in the tri-state area is going to know sooner or later," Ronnie broke in. She then explained what she and her attorney had discussed. "I'm demanding a court trial, and suing for indignities!"

"Good girl," C.J. answered. "I'll try and make sure beyond a shadow of a doubt that you get whatever you need." C.J. hurriedly wrote something on a napkin and when lunch had ended he passed it over to Rhonda. "Read this later," he said. She folded the napkin and placed it in her purse.

"As they were leaving the restaurant C.J. looked at his childhood friend and the tone of his voice was very gruff. He sounded very upset and agitated as he spoke. "You really dropped a bomb on me Ronnie! Let me get some guys to do a number on him . . . just for fun. They won't kill him or the girls, just rough them up a bit. Scare the hell out of them."

"No C.J.," she answered. "I'm playing to win. We can do it with technology and your connections. They can eat their own shit and I don't care who gets hurt in the process. No one gave any consideration to me or to my son's feelings and this time I'm getting even."

C.J. kissed her on the cheek and told her he would be in touch. As he walked across the parking lot, Rhonda knew his mind would not rest until things were settled with her. She had confidence in C.J. He would make sure she would win this private little war! He had come to her rescue her as a child, and she had never forgotten. In her heart she just knew.

As she got in the car her old friend named pain began to surface its ugly head again and she was getting nauseated. It started to rain. *Even the angel's cry,* she thought. The rain was now gently falling from the sky!

"Thank you God, for C.J. today," she spoke out loud while driving home. She then tried to recall the chapter of Psalms she had read before going to sleep the night before. She had opened the Bible, a gift, from her parents on her wedding day. It fell open to Psalm 18: 4-6[10]. She read it aloud and cried. Like David, the servant of the Lord who talked the words that delivered him from the hands of all his enemies, she knew her life was sinking fast. Bridges would be burned and sometimes, no matter the cost, things are broken that can never be repaired. Life for her and the boys would never be quite the same again. Joel's choices had forever changed the paths for so many and he didn't even realize it. "I feel sorry for you Joel. Today I even feel sorry for the stupid whores that think you are so wonderful. Real happiness comes from inside, not from someone else. I fear I may have learned that lesson too late. I was a fool to put you first in my life. I knew God never put you in charge but I loved you so much. I couldn't see beyond who I thought you were. Do I still love you? Can I? How could you think so little of me? Why?"

As Rhonda slowly pulled into the driveway, she picked up the mail. Before entering the house, she pulled out a large envelope from the phone company. As she continued to look through the pile of mail, she removed a second letter addressed to her by hand with no return address. *Probably another note from one of his women. She opened neither envelope but placed them in her purse. Tomorrow is another day. I can't handle anymore now.*

---

[10] The sorrows of death compassed me, and the floods of ungodly men made me afraid. The sorrows of hell compassed me about: the snares of death prevented me. In my distress I called upon the Lord, and cried unto my God: he heard my voice out of his temple, and my cry came before him, even into his ears.

Slowly she reached for the napkin C.J. had written on, took her pain medication and proceeded to her room. In silence, she undressed and got into bed. She began to read C.J.'s note and drifted off to sleep. The combination of pain medication and emotional exhaustion always made her tired. The note read as follows:

Ron, I can't remember who wrote this but it helped me when I was in your situation. I think it was Barry Manilow. Really the author is unknown. Love, C.J.

Bach gave us God's word;(that we might communicate)
Mozart gave us God's laughter;(that we might enjoy the communication)
Beethoven gave us God's fire;(as a torch in the night), but when all else fails
God gave us music that we might pray without words.
Forgive, forget, get better!

Chapter Six

Two days later the phone rang. Rhonda did not pick up until she heard C.J.'s voice on the answering machine. Just like a private eye to call when you look your worst" she spoke out loud before picking up the receiver.

"Hi Ron. Is Joel Around?"

"No," she stated without emotion.

"Good. I'll be right out."

While she waited for C. J. Rhonda put on a pot of coffee to perk and went into the bathroom to put on lipstick so that she would not look so bad. As she exited the bathroom, the door bell rang. When Rhonda opened the door, C.J. entered with a suitcase. "We'll fix their asses," he said. "Today we begin the pay back." Rhonda looked in amazement at the small devices he unpacked, there were all these small metal gadgets with wires that she didn't even know existed. Quickly he took all the phone receivers apart and placed 12 hour voice activated recorders in each one. While doing this, he asked why Joel's car was in the driveway. "Joe picked him up this morning to go on a golf outing," Rhonda said.

"Perfect" he answered. "See this," he was holding a small device no larger than a fifty-cent piece. "This one is a recorder and lets me know the exact location of his vehicle." "You got keys to everything?"

"Yes!" She was getting excited. She walked outside with him and watched as he placed the small devices up under the seats of the cars and the van. "No one will ever know they are there."

"Are you sure?"

"Trust me on this kid. It's my lively hood. I have a clientele list you wouldn't believe."

"But I need pictures too!" The excitement in Rhonda's voice was coming through loud and clear.

"First things first, love. I'll get what you need. When I'm done with old Joel and his women, you will be able to have a field day."

"The firm that cleans Joel's office just happens to have someone working there that helps me out occasionally. Tonight I'll have his office phone fixed and I'll even get copies of all the faxes . . . in and out. Technology is a great tool now days. Nothing is private if you know the right people.

There are even guys he golfs and works with whose names I've managed to get... just waiting to see him take a fall. Even his so-called friends think he's full of himself. He's a power mad son of a bitch that intimidates everyone by yelling to get his own way. You wouldn't believe what people will tell you. His wonderful lady friends can't keep their mouths shut either. People always have to tell someone. It makes them feel big or something. Just chock it up to human nature. I have girls that only go to bars to collect information. Hell, his best friend told me he was an ass hole. He said he always thought Joel was a cut above the rest until he found out he was cheating on his wife. His words were, to quote him, 'He's no better than the rest of us bastards out there... probably worse! Everyone knows we cheat. He's lost a lot of respect in the ranks. Hell! He's no better than we are. You can't look up to nobody these days."

"They don't have the nerve to tell him to his face though, I'd bet. They all laugh and talk to him and tell him what he wants to hear. He could make life miserable for them, you know. Behind his back it's a different story. Hell, I even got addresses and phone numbers of where the women work.

I know exactly what they do besides screwing around with Joel. These people are nuts and they think he's flipped out... so this should give you an idea of how really crazy they all are. One guy named Charley is really getting his rocks off over this whole thing with Joel and Cassie. Hell, she screwed Charley over so bad. He paid to send her to some technical computer school so she could supposedly take care of her kids. His old lady dumped him. All at once, Cassie has a job and is back living with that last husband of hers. Men talk as much as women these days. Buy them a few drinks and you can get a book full of information on almost any given day. Know what I'm sayen? Before it's all done , I'll get pictures, locations and, well . . . You'll be surprised what I come up with."

"He's going on a four-day golf trip next weekend," Rhonda said.

"Good!" said C.J. "Bet I can get some great pictures. Let me know any details you find out and I'll have someone on it guaranteed."

"I've taken care of the car phones and I have someone following the three girls and him. We'll pick up and record all conversations. This could get interesting! If I catch him in a motel or hotel with one of them, I'll break the door down if you want but we'll have to pay for it of course."

"Gee, I don't know," Rhonda answered.

"Well I won't if I don't have to," he said. "These new tiny cameras can get great pictures through cracks, in dark vehicles and even through draperies sometimes. And these new recorders are powerful enough to record the conversation even if you're outside the room. We can even drill a small hole from an adjoining room and get what we need. The motel managers don't even realize it. Both the drills and cameras are so quiet and so small, no one even notices. We can patch them in minutes and no one is the wiser.

Got to run, kid, but don't worry. Believe me. I've seen it all before. They're so busy planning ways to sneak around. They'll never believe you could catch them."

With that, C.J. left as quickly as he came. For a few minutes, Rhonda felt at peace with the world. *I'll play the game your way Joel. But I fully intend to win. I've recognized the problem at last. I have calmly evaluated the situation, explored my options and we're going to live with my solution. I am taking control of my life. I might be expendable to you Joel, but you'll never forget who I am, the crazy old stupid bitch , as you love to call me, created by your own hand.*

In the months that followed, C.J. made good on his word. He delivered faxes, motel tapes, phone tapes, car tapes, and pictures that made Rhonda physically sick to look at. He even took the time to make sure there were four copies of everything, one for her, one for K. Stephen Sawyer, one for her safety deposit box and an extra . . . just in case.

One night C.J. called Cassie's house and told her husband. Of course, we figured that she managed to lie about it to her husband and convince him it was just a nasty prank because she hurriedly called Joel the next morning at the office. Rhonda found the tape funny when she heard it. Joel of course came home furious and screaming. He had assured Cassie there were no pictures. No one was that smart. Besides they had been careful. When he left, Rhonda phoned C.J. to get the address and drove to Cassie's house. She was not there, however, her husband talked to Rhonda. He told her that he was a victim, just like she was. Strange statement she thought! He believed his wife. They had just renewed their wedding vows last year and he trusted her completely. When Cassie drove up, she hesitated before getting out of the car. Fear was on her face. She told Rhonda that Joel was a very close friend and a WONDERFUL boss! Had anyone mentioned her name when they had called she wanted to know. Rhonda lied and said no. In twenty-nine years only one other girl had ever told her Joel was a wonderful boss! He was having an affair with her also. The bell went off in Rhonda's head. She remembered when little Connie, a cute angel faced tiny blonde, worked for Joel when the boys were small. She was always giving Joel little gifts and letting him drive her car. Eventually everything escalated to the point where she wanted more and more. Joel tried to dump her but she would not be dumped. That angel, as Joel always referred to her as, had really tried to give Rhonda a way to go. Rhonda never told Joel that she knew about that affair. The attorney Rhonda worked for at the time took care of everything very quietly. Joel always thought he had just managed to dump her with no problem. Rhonda knew better. Finally poor Connie managed to snag someone else, got married and eventually changed jobs. Everyone always said what a terror Joel was to work for, even people that liked him personally. Cassie was lying and Rhonda was not surprised. She thanked them for their time. *You poor sap,* she thought driving home. *You are married to a whore and don't even know it!* Cassie's phone number was changed the next day.

72

When Joel came home, she told him she had gone to Cassie's and assured them there were no detectives or pictures. She was so sorry that their family problems had involved them. Joel seemed sufficiently satisfied and the taped conversation between him and Cassie the next day proved they thought they were getting away with the lies they thought had been performed perfectly. "Give him enough rope and he'll hang himself," Joe and Park had told her. She had taught them well she thought proudly. Some things I taught them did sink in after all!

Rhonda's condition was deteriorating and she knew it better than anyone! Life had taken so much out of her. But there was still one more item to address before she left this world. It probably was crazy but she wanted to get the house painted on the outside one last time. Rhonda resolved to get this done as quickly as possible. However, the disease was taking more of her energy. When night finally fell, she prayed. This was indeed the toughest fight of her life! It was getting harder all the time trying to deal with her own mortality, Joel's betrayal and keep her faith. She found herself talking to God so often it seemed. She often wondered if he really was listening to her. Maybe she was so busy thinking and trying to figure the situation out, the whys and who's, that she was totally caught up in telling him her problems. Perhaps she was not listening to the things God was trying to convey to her. She only knew that her days were numbered. She needed to find the strength to complete the tasks at hand. Joel's circle had to include the boys after she was gone. They would be the only ones left that would truly care when he could no longer take care of himself.

She recalled an e-mail from a friend, sent to her quite a few years back when she herself had been going through difficult times. Jane had been such a strong person. Life was so precious to her. " If things don't kill you they make you stronger, Jane had written. So pray for me, please. I am desperately trying to hate what someone does and still find it my heart to love the person. This is the hardest task I have ever experienced." Rhonda had taken time to respond, not knowing what the correct response might be except to say she would remember her in her daily prayers. Every once in awhile that e-mail would just for some unknown reason, pop into her head. It was kind of haunting but was something Rhonda had never forgotten. On one occasion she had shared it with the boys. Park reminded her of it once in awhile when things seemed to be at their worst. Park and Joel were over comers. Thank God. That e-mail surfaced in Rhonda's mind at the strangest times. Funny, the things you relate to a person after they are gone.

Quite often she would find herself wondering about the strangest things. How much difference was there between sanity and insanity? Am I insane, or is it sane to become numb to the suffering of others? Is it sane to feel to deeply? Do the souls of the sane bleed in the same way that the souls of the insane bleed? Do the souls of the sane ever bleed?

Are the people we class as the insane ones just driven by incomprehensible grief over all the conditions that exist in the world in which they are forced to live. Are the insane unable to change the circumstances around them or do they make the choice not to deal with it? Do choices bring change, or because of change are we forced to make choices? Don't you wonder if these people really are the insane ones of our society? It is most interesting to note that somehow and I do not understand the whys or the how of it all, except, facts point to most of them always recognizing their own ability to make things right. I can't help wondering how and why. The guidelines of life, have become so tangled due to change or choice it seems. Perhaps everyone becomes insane at some point in time and we as a society refuse to deal with it. Accepting it as the norm is easier and much less complicated. So who is insane?

Was that why mama had always stressed love and forgiveness? Forgiveness is an easier word to say than to actually mean and put to real practical use. Once again, however, Rhonda only knew to pray. She also made a mental note to remember to ask mama if there was any mental illness back in the family tree somewhere.

It's me again, Lord. I did not ask Cassie about the in excess of 34 phone calls per week she had been making to Joel. I just came home. Please Lord, let me finish what I have started, just fifteen more minutes in the sun is all I ask. I'm tired and weary, but some people, if just once in awhile, have to stand up for what they believe in. The younger generation , otherwise ,will never be taught or understand that everyone pays for choices in life.

I know vengeance only belongs to you but please let me have the fun of making them all squirm a little before I go. I feel such great sorrow for them, even knowing they feel no guilt and will not address what has been done with any honesty. Please Lord, be merciful and change the course of their lives so they will once again renew their friendship with you. Surely among the lot, one will tell the truth. Please help me Lord ... I'm so tired anymore . . ..

Rhonda fell asleep without finishing her conversation with God that night. Nor did the angel of death come to her door.

Chapter Seven

Morning arrived and Rhonda felt much to her surprise, refreshed. After downing her morning pills and coffee, she actually felt like facing the world.

She had noticed the white paint was beginning to peel on the outside of the house. "This place is starting to look like a shack, Thor." Rhonda was talking to the large black Doberman which had been a birthday gift to her nearly ten years ago from Joel. Thor hurried to Rhonda's side as quickly as his old bones would permit to receive a pat on the head. The sound of his name always brought him to her. "Good boy," she said as she patted the top of his head. "Mommy is going to give Daddy a big surprise!" Rhonda walked into the den and picked up the phone directory. "There you are," she spoke as if someone was actually, in the room, listening to her. She quickly dialed the number. "Hi Mike. This is Rhonda Smith. I'm feeling fine today thanks. How have you been?"

After the formalities were concluded, she proceeded to tell him that she wanted to surprise Joel and have the house painted over the weekend while he would be out of town. Mike Jantec was a local painter and previously had painted the Smith house in addition to countless others in the area over the years. He was often referred to as being the greatest vocal newspaper in three counties. Mike loved to talk. He told everyone he came in contact with any news he knew. This morning was no different.

"Sure, Rhonda... It will cost a little more to have it done on a weekend ya know. It's tough to get painters on the weekend. You would think everyone these days is independently wealthy.

By the way, have you gone down Maple Street lately? You have to see the Lotousky house. I just finished over there. Brenda insisted that George let her pick out the colors. Ended up I painted it sage green with light creme trim. Then, would you believe, she added a third color which turned out to be brown. She said it needed to look a bit more colorful for some damnable reason! Actually, it turned out to look pretty nice.

"I suppose you've already heard... she's been running around with her boss. Everyone in town has been talking about her antics. And poor George, all he does is work so he can give her anything she wants. Pity isn't it? I hear she ran around on her first husband too. People talk ya know. Oh well, these days, I guess nothing is sacred. Are you changing the color of the house? I can send someone over with samples." Mike continued without ever taking a breath.

"Yes I am, but samples won't be necessary. I want you to paint the house black."

"Did you say black?" The tone in Mike's voice sounded as if he had just gone into shock.

"Yes I did." Rhonda spoke very calmly. "Would you mind sending someone over with a gallon of paint later today so I can try it on something? I want a real special look. The trim is to be white but the main structure is to be black. I do not want charcoal. It must be black. The darker the better."

"I'll send a boy over later. If that is okay with you? Hold on a minute"

Rhonda could hear him talking to someone named Larry. When he came back on the line, he told her one of his summer workers would be getting off at noon and would drop by with the paint and a brush so she could try it on a board or something.

About twelve thirty, a tall, lean, dark-haired boy rang the door bell. "I'm Larry. Mike asked me to drop this off on my way home." The teenager was in his work clothes. Rhonda smiled and asked him to leave the paint on the porch by the door.

Just as he was about to leave, she called to him. "Hey Larry, do you know of anyone that would like to make a quick twenty bucks for very little work this afternoon?"

"Doing what?"

"I want someone to stripe off the house in black, a couple of boards on the front and side so everyone will be able to see it as they drive by. If it takes more time than I think it will, I will pay a little more."

"Heck, for a fast twenty, I'll do it for you. Would it be okay if I called my mom to let her know that I will be a little late?"

"Sure thing," she said as she handed the portable phone out the door. In less than an hour, the door bell rang. Larry asked Rhonda if she would mind taking a look at the house to see if he was finished. Rhonda walked around both the front and the side that was visible to the street below, checking out the new color. "Perfect, exactly what the doctor ordered." Rhonda reached into her jean pocket, pulled out a twenty-dollar bill and handed it to Larry. "You did a great job, exactly what I had in mind."

"Thanks, Mrs. Smith. I'll wash out the brush and get going then."

"Thank you for doing the job for me." Rhonda knew Joel would be angry. In a small town, everyone notices the least little change. She was banking on it. Joel was leaving for another golf weekend tomorrow. He would, therefore, get to see what she had done on this wonderful Wednesday afternoon before he left town.

Sure enough, he entered the house screaming at her. "You're crazy, you stupid bitch! You have really lost it Rhonda! I should have you committed.! You are nuts! What the hell is wrong with you? It's going to cost me plenty to have Mike come over and undo the mess you have made! You are getting crazier by the day! Who the hell would want to come home to someone as crazy as you are? There is not one ounce of common sense left in that stupid brain of yours! I hope the cancer kills you soon! You are crazy! Bonkers! A classic nut case! Do you understand? You are nothing! Nuts! Crazy!" Joel was screaming so loudly now that old Thor was cowering and trying to get as close to Rhonda as he could.

Rhonda did not move but remained very calm without the slightest hint of any emotion in her voice and said, " You are absolutely right, Joel. I am crazy, crazier than even you know, so don't forget it. I want you to tell that to the judge. After all, a crazy woman cannot possibly take care of herself, now can she? You made me crazy. You turned me into what I am now and you don't seem to like what you have created. I would rather be hated for what I am, than to be loved for something I'm not"

"You and your dam cliches' make me sick, you bitch! I'm leaving for the weekend as soon as I can get packed! I sure as hell don't want to stay around here and listen to a lunatic!"

"Why not? Your bimbos have to be real nut cases. Think about it! If I was going to screw around, it certainly would not be with some old married man. I'd want some hard body a little younger banging my bones. Women are no different from men, if they are going to play around! She's not having intercourse with you, Joel. She's plain fucking your bank account, your retirement money and everything else you'll give her or she thinks that she is going to get for the favors she gives you! Only a real nut case gives it away for free! Don't let the door hit you in the ass on the way out!"

She was now totally exhausted. When she awoke the house was dark and it was evening. Joel was gone and Thor was sleeping on the floor at her feet. Rhonda sat up in the dark quiet room and let her thoughts drift into things she believed and what she would like to change in her life if she could.

She and Joel had little contact with each other. It seemed that they could not be in the same room beyond hello or they were tearing each other apart. " Why can't I just ignore what he says and practice what Father Bill told me to do instead of permitting him to set my mood. I always open my mouth in anger and give him reasons to do what he does. Lord knows he doesn't need my help. He is perfectly capable of thinking up his own excuses. You have to help me to work on that, Lord." The only one to hear her besides the God above was Thor.

Rhonda had a rather strange belief system that she kept for the most part to herself. She truly believed that life was really a test. Most people have so much busy in their life that they never take the time to get in touch with themselves or address moral issues. These people just run through life and die. Reincarnation was something that she had never fully ruled out. All people pass through one's life for a reason she thought. The purpose had to be either to teach something or to learn something. In her mind, if the parties involved did not learn a lesson about life they would be forced to take the same test over and over again, until they did learn. Perhaps some never learn in one lifetime as we know it. The unfortunate non-learners would have to come back and take the same tests over again with the same people. Next time around, however, the creator had the power to change your gender, social status, and relationship with that same soul in order for you to learn, pass the test and grow. With each test passed, you became stronger and elevated closer to God. She felt that she was a very old soul and in her former life had been a woman of power and substance. It seemed apparent to her that she must have inflicted a lot of pain upon others. This time around it was her turn to find out exactly what the wrath inflicted by others felt like. She had always been a fighter and doubted if she was learning what she was supposed to this time either, nonetheless, she always held out hope. How many times will I have to do this to get it right, was a question she often asked herself? "Thank you for the thorn." she spoke out loud. "Without Joel, I would not have been forced to grow and turn to you. Is this the lesson I am supposed to learn this time around? I always knew you were there, but figured you had more important things to worry about. I always felt that you expected me to handle my own problems. This time , however, I don't seem to be able to handle it alone. I am sure you get tired of listening to me but I really need your help!"

Her thoughts drifted back to the paint color she had chosen for the house. She had always thought the legislature should address and pass laws more geared to the lifestyles of the general population. Everyone is so caught up in where they live and the color of their next door neighbor.

Do I live on the right or the wrong side of the tracks? Society has always painted themselves into boxes. Instead of worrying what color skin your next door neighbor has, one should be more concerned with what he or she is. Our neighborhoods are defined by mundane items such as race, rich, poor, upperclass, middle class, and lower class. It seems no one has ever really had the foresight or the integrity to seek out a new direction. It could easily be handled by legislating the color of house you live in or the car you own.

The possibilities are limitless. Car colors could even be used to define what you do for a living. One could then make the choice of where they wanted to live determined by the colors they saw there.

Rhonda, it seemed, had always danced to the tune of a different drummer. She had decided a long time ago that society forced people into being sneaks. She felt prostitution should be legalized, taxed and operated as any profitable business governed by health controls. In her mind, society would be more accepting of the fact that Janie went to work as a prostitute at such and such a place every day, made a decent living, paid taxes and was disease free. She could lay there all day long and tell each Jon how much she loved him and get paid. All male prostitutes would fall under the same guidelines. After all, there are lots of housewives out there as well as husbands who are stupidly giving it away for free. Prostitutes having enough smarts to simply charge for the service are not given any respect and fined heavily if caught. In Rhonda's eyes there was something wrong with this picture. We cannot legislate morality, so legalizing prostitution would certainly be better then taking a chance on disease and could put a dent in divorce due to adultery as well as generate more money for the general fund. The pecking order would be in place once again. Jobs for everyone!

She once asked a neighbor of hers that was having an indiscreet affair with the mail carrier, if either one of them had asked the other about former sexual partners, or a health certificate? "Just because someone looks clean and smells good doesn't mean they are not carrying a disease that could be transmitted to you during that few minutes of foreplay or intimacy." Bonnie had laughed at Rhonda that day and shrugged her shoulders.

"Most people involved in affairs never use condoms or any other means of protection. You are crazy, Bonnie. You have become just like a bitch in heat. You can't wait for Mr. Wonderful to bang that sweet spot!" It turned out that Mr. Wonderful just happened to get the same venereal disease as Bonnie, his wife, Bonnie's husband and the cute little waitress that just happened to live two blocks over. Who gave it to whom?

When Marti told Rhonda about this latest bit of town news, Rhonda recalled the conversation she had with Bonnie a few months back. " I sure hope the do gooders in town don't get wind of this, and put two and two together," she told Marti. " Next, the U.S. mail will be subject to decontamination chambers!"

"You are a trip Ron, leave it to you to think of that," Marti chuckled.

"I will certainly ask the mail carrier where his hands have been before I will take a letter from him tomorrow," Rhonda laughed.

"I think the whole town should be tested."

"You know, that sounds like a great idea, Marti. If we are going to start a crusade I think we should first rent a billboard. NEWTON FALLS RESIDENTS GET TESTED! We can phone the local t.v. and radio stations. It could even go national!

We should insist everyone have their DNA checked as well. The results of that would be fascinating since DNA is something no one can wash away. If you have had sexual contact with a certain someone it stays with you forever. I wonder why the legislature doesn't pass a law requiring it to be a mandatory test in all divorce cases caused by adultery? It could save the courts a ton of money."

"Why? Because everything including the legislature is run by men. Doesn't that tell you something?"

"Yeah. We should run for office! We could start our own party and call it the F.A.R.T. Party (females are running tests). Our platform could be based on everything that's considered politically incorrect and no one has the guts to address. DNA tests for everyone, over the age of fifteen!"

"Sounds good to me, but I can't get started today. I have two perms to put in this afternoon!"

"I am pretty busy myself. But we could call C.J. and have him get the ball rolling!"

Both had laughed, enjoying the moment!

On the day the invitation arrived, each of the three girls was flying sky high after opening it. Their thoughts, ironically, had all been the same! I am someone special! Joel is willing to take the chance on losing his family and wife for little ole me! I wonder if he has finally told her about us and how much we mean to each other. How lucky can I get!? He needs me and believes I need him so she is finally out of the picture!

Each one vacillated on and on. I wonder if she has left the house? Will he ask me to move in? Should I tell my husband now or wait? Each justified their actions with the thought that if he really loved Rhonda, he wouldn't have been out running around on her to begin with. Every thought was followed by another. The excitement was building inside each of them as each looked forward to the impending fateful luncheon. What will I wear? Should I arrive early or late? Did he buy me something? Should I act surprised? I don't want it to appear that I have no feelings for poor Rhonda. Each made a mental note to tell him that she never meant for anyone to get hurt. After all, it was something that just happened. Neither one was to blame for the circumstances at hand! The heart wants what the heart wants. We just happen to be among the few willing to bite the bullet and go for it! One thought only generated another and another.

"I never intended for it to happen, Joel." Each girl practiced the line in her head. If Rhonda can't hold on to him and keep him happy, that is her problem! I wonder what he is going to tell me? I knew sooner or later he would leave her for me.

All three girls arrived at the same time and entered the restaurant. No one spoke. Each had her own private thoughts on what was about to transpire on this happiest of days. Looking extremely happy, each took a seat at a vacant table to wait for Joel. Jimmy cordially greeted the girls as he escorted each to their own table. After seating each girl he presented her with a long stemmed rose tied with a lovely white ribbon. There were two words embossed in large gold letters upon the flowing streamers. HAPPINESS IS

Annie and Jimmy greeted Rhonda with hugs and kisses as usual. Jimmy told her that the flowers had been delivered and he had given them to the ladies as she had requested.

"Is my Marti coming?"

"No, Annie, not today. This is strictly a business luncheon."

"What kind of business do you got with the likes of them?" Annie spoke and nodded her head toward the dining room.

Rhonda grinned. Her head was held high. The black silk dress fell gracefully in place against her small frame. She felt good about the way she looked and it was showing. Rhonda planned to seize the moment with the intent of pushing the envelope as far as it would go today.

Each of the three girls was sitting alone at a table with a rose in front of her! "Nice touch," she said aloud as she approached the dining area.

The dining area was empty of patrons. It was almost 1:30 in the afternoon.

Rhonda called each name out loud. "Cassie, Jan, Cindy," each girl looked up startled. "Please join me girls. I'm so glad to see you received your roses!" Each had a look of surprise and horror at the same time. "Joel won't be coming today …surprise!" She said laughing.

Each girl edged slowly toward Rhonda's table not quite knowing what to expect. Suddenly Cassie shot her foul mouth off. "I'm not sitting with you bitch, now or ever!"

Rhonda calmly turned to her with eyes of steel. Looking through her not at her.

"Sit down, Cassie. Sit down and shut up, or you won't be going to a happy home tonight."

"You threatening me, you bitch?" she shouted back in Rhonda's face.

"If you have to ask, you are dumber than I gave you credit for," Rhonda stated flatly. "But I assure you, it's not a threat. I never threaten, sweetie. If I say it you can bank on it!"

Cassie flopped back in her chair while Jan and Cindy looked on in shock. They were no longer even smiling, just easing into their chairs without uttering a word, forgetting the black long stemmed rose that each had waiting for them when they were seated.

Rhonda felt like she was on a roll. She walked over to each table gingerly picking up each flower and laid one in front of each of the girls. "Wouldn't want you to forget the lovely flowers, girls? Joel's money bought them and he would be very upset if his wife were not hospitable. Happiness is doing what is right. Right?" No one responded.

Jimmy handed Rhonda a menu. "Please bring the salad specials and an order of garlic bread for each of us." Rhonda stated the order precisely until ordering the beverages, then Rhonda looked up from the menu. "You all do drink coffee, I presume. Or would anyone rather have a beer or how about tea?" No one answered; instead they all sat glaring at each other and then at Rhonda. "Coffee for all of us." Jimmy left with the order. Suddenly Jan snapped at Rhonda.

"You cannot force us to calmly sit here and take your shit, Mrs. Smith."

Rhonda looked across the table and smiled broadly. "Now, now girls; Let's conduct ourselves as ladies. Please try and refrain from trying to add insult to injury. We all break a law now and then. Some of us break God's laws, others break mans law. So sue me!" Rhonda smiled. "It's my party...my rules!" she said while adjusting her purse on her lap. "I have a loaded 38 in my purse, and a permit to carry a concealed weapon. Now tell me does anyone have a problem with that? I guess Joel forgot to mention the fact that I am one hell of a shot." Rhonda spoke deliberately, slowly, calmly and quietly. "We are going to have a nice lunch girls and we are not going to leave before I tell you the luncheon is adjourned. I trust, I have made myself clear."

No one moved. Rhonda continued. "First let me tell you how it really is. Don't you wonder somewhere in those tiny little heads why this crazy woman is holding you here for lunch with a gun? I have cancer. Know what that is? The big 'C?' No reply came forth. " To make a long story short, I will be dead in the near future. You all know what dead is, right? So, if anyone here believes I have anything to lose, I would classify you as an idiot."

"I have no marriage. In fact, beyond my dignity, there is not much left. I have Nothing! Nothing, that is, except for my sons. Both of whom think I should do anything that makes me personally feel good. If any one of you don't like that, I'll be glad to tell you: that's your fucking problem!" Slowly she took a cigarette from the pack she was holding. The tone of her voice changed as she once again was smiling broadly. "I do have him!" The girls were now staring, with a look that can only be described as shock. Rhonda was holding the cigarette gently above her head for all to see. "This little fellow is my lover! He is always there when I need him. He doesn't have a wife! Actually he can be very stimulating and at times I find him very satisfying. The best thing about him is the fact that he never gives me any shit! He doesn't lie or cheat! Quite remarkable for a lover, wouldn't you agree, even if he isn't really politically correct!"

Rhonda lit a cigarette and jokingly said, "I would offer one but I know none of you would ever suck on such filth. I'm sure you're all really very careful of what you put in your mouth!. Somewhere down the line all of you, or perhaps it was Joel, screwed up royally."

"We don't have to take this shit from you Mrs. Smith," Cassie hissed. "This is unlawful restraint and I'm going to the police."

"Then get up and go. Test me. If you continue to screw with me, you're a bigger fool than I thought. You have everything to lose. I have nothing to lose at all. Nothing! You girls have heard the saying before I'm sure. Only in your world it kind of goes 'Wear nothing at all,' doesn't it?" Rhonda laughed.

They each sat nervously, glaring at Rhonda and at each other, like school children not knowing if they had to raise their hand to be excused.

The salads arrived as did the garlic toast and coffee.

"Enjoy! Think of this as a last meal. You all know who Judas was, don't you? We'll have lunch and talk." Rhonda smiled wide as she winked at Cassie in particular.

"First, we should all get to know each other. Let's start with our name, then number of children. Move on to number of husbands and, how could I forget, how long married. You're all bedding down my husband. Therefore, everyone should get to know their competition. This will be so…much fun! If you want to compare notes or anything else, feel free to share!

"This is going to be important, not only in the next step of our relationship, but for my own personal information. And it'll allow you to find out how smart each other is. You know my motto? Let's make the playing field level. After all, it's all in the spirit of fun!" The three women were barely touching the salad. "Oh, come now. Eat up!" Rhonda chided. "What's wrong? No one hungry? Perhaps you would like to send your lunch back and chose another entrée'." No one answered. Silence once again flooded the room.

"Okay then. I'll introduce each of you since the cat seems to have your tongues. You can call me Rhonda. This is Cassie, Jan, and last but not least Cindy. So you know, Cindy has the biggest star! You do know what that means, I hope. Now, is everyone ready to continue with the introductions?"

Rhonda looked from face to face. Rhonda's guests appeared to be paralyzed. They looked as if either they were on a Soma holiday or had just been frightened to death! Rhonda ,however, was having the time of her life! They barely even dared to breathe. There was only silence, awkward silence. And Rhonda reveled in the uneasy silence.

"No? Well, since no one wants to begin, I'll tell each of you about the others.

Cassie is currently married to Frank. Her forth marriage! Actually, that's twice to Frank. She has four kids, one dog and drives a cute red sports utility vehicle. Wears her clothing too tight and attends aerobics on Thursdays, after which she calls Joel on the car phone and drives to their special place, MacDonalds. He picks her up there, springs for a coke, and you can guess the rest for yourself.

"Oh, and she is so proud of her big silicone boobs. She just goes from one affair to another, always pretending it is the first time. Right Cass?

She is impressed with the love of power, money and social standing in the community and plans to get it if she has to bed every boss that she has in order to get what she wants. I guess you all have the same mind set. I am sure you can understand.

Jan is divorced, loafs at Sundowns, drinks beer, lives in a mobile home. She's your basic trailer trash specimen, the kind of woman you might see on that *Cops* t.v. show late at night. She's got a real cutesy answering machine message. Sucks life from the system and is an ex-teacher. Here's the real catcher . . . she thinks she's built like a brick shit house. All she does is work on that round little bottom she's so proud of! Her last husband, Don was it, left her because she was having an affair with her new boss? Fed up with her antics he finally filed for divorce. She is trying to screw herself from rags to riches, and is as easy as they come. Joel only gives her one little star in his secret little black book. We can assume the star is only for effort!

Ah, Cindy. I saved darling little Cindy for last. Cindy's husband died. She owns a house and was left a substantial amount of money, works at Bevas gym as a receptionist, plays golf, and if I might add, has two grown daughters. She loves her dry wrinkled face. She was looking for husband number 2 long before number 1 died. In fact, she has been trying to hitch herself to Joel for a long time now. She even promoted Joel right in front of me many times in the last twenty nine years. There is not an ounce of shame in her skinny bony body, and not a brain in her head.

I have lots more information on each of you along with pictures of each of you in very compromising positions with my soon to be ex-husband. I've got pictures from a weekend in Meadowview. That was supposed to be a golf weekend. Sound familiar to anyone here? I've got pictures from the Holiday Motel, the Ravin Hotel and lots of others in both my ole man's company car and the "pecker mobile." Oh, I'm sorry. I mean the van. I have pictures from McDonald's. You name it, sweetheart, and odds are I've got it somewhere in my files. I even have pictures of one of you in his office, behind closed locked doors. Technology certainly is great these days, don't you agree?"

"Now let me ask each of you. Do you really like bedding married men?" Rhonda laughed. She laughed so hard it was unsettling. No one answered. "Is mine really that good? I do not have a comparison chart here but wondered how you rated these guys."

"Answer me!" Rhonda stopped laughing to echo her demand. Each one of the women looked startled but managed to choke out a strangled "No."

"This is what you are going to do for me because I bought you lunch."Rhonda now spoke as if she were a boss and giving orders to a group of workers. While she was speaking she reached into her purse and pulled out a packet of pictures. She began passing the pictures around the table.

Jimmy arrived with more coffee and the entrees just as each girl was silently gazing at a picture of herself or one of the other girls in very comprising positions with Joel. There were nude shots, bed shots, butt shots, kissing shots and many more pictures that Rhonda found too distasteful for most ladies to imagine. Jimmy placed the entrees down and exited the dining area without ever speaking a word.

He glanced at Rhonda and disappeared from sight hustling back to the kitchen. "Rhonda's really got her dander up today, Annie. Me, I'm not going back in there until those women leave."

"If Ronnie wants dessert she'll let us know." Annie spoke without ever looking up from the table where she sat peeling potatoes for the evening crowd.

"I am giving each of you a card with the name and phone number of my attorney on it. You will go there after calling, to find out a mutually convenient time and sign papers for me to use in court admitting to the fact that you indeed are having sexual contact with my husband. For this favor I will not have you subpoenaed to court, nor will your names be brought up for the public at large to know for sure that you are involved in any way. If you refuse, you will have your day in court along with Joel. Your alternate choice is to be charged with indignities, which I am certainly able to prove. I would advise you to sign the papers. Simple, short and sweet!" As she spoke Rhonda never flinched. Her voice was articulate, clear and demanding, indeed a voice of authority.

Cassie spoke first. "This is blackmail, You goddamn bitch!"

"Call it whatever makes you the most comfortable, dear. I prefer to call it a choice. Does anyone else care to add anything to this wonderful luncheon?" Jan and Cindy just sat there, hands shaking, glaring at Rhonda and each other.

"Better eat up, girls. We wouldn't want anyone to think we had so much business to take care of that we barely touched lunch, now would we?"

"I will not sign anything without first consulting a lawyer," Cindy said. She finally managed to find the courage to speak.

"Consult the Pope if you want to. I could care less. Feel free to take as many of the photos with you as you like. I have duplicates and plenty of other ones if I need them. I also have faxes, taped phone conversations, notes, itemized motel and phone bills and proof of all phone calls in and out of my house, Joel's mobile phone, and office phones, whatever you want!"

"None of which is admissible in court!" Jan was now speaking, almost yelling.

"Good girl, Jan! Perhaps yes, perhaps no. But who can say when and where these things might surface? This type of material could cause a lot of questions to arise. Why families could be turned upside down, careers ruined, and lives made one living hell. You know what I mean? I am more than certain the Judge and Joel's attorney will have a field day viewing and listening to such delightful bits of information. There certainly will be no question as to why I am in court." Rhonda's ice cold eyes were looking straight into Jan's now worried face. "A thought just came to mind and I wondered if any one of you can intelligently answer it for me? How can you demand and expect right choices from your children and your spouses when each one of you can't seem to make correct choices concerning your own behavior? You are certainly great role models, aren't you?

Are there any other doubts or questions any one of you would like me to answer? If not, you are all free to go. I am not springing for dessert. I've been told by someone very near and dear to each of you how sweet you all are!" Now she was taunting them and enjoying it so!

Suddenly the tone of her voice went from butter would melt in your mouth to that of a truck driver. "You have exactly five days from today to make up your minds and sign those papers for me! Make no mistake! I will file charges against each of you for a sizeable amount, and fully intend to win. This, my dears, concludes lunch! I sincerely hope that it was as good for you as it was for me!"

"You are crazier than hell!" Cassie yelled back as she was leaving.

"Right you are! Crazy, but not stupid, there is a difference, you know!"

The other two girls followed quickly behind Cassie. "Life certainly can be a bitch at times. They all are bedding the same man and will not even acknowledge each other." Rhonda muttered to herself.

She quickly went to the kitchen, kissed Annie and Jimmy, thanked them for being so hospitable, paid the bill and went directly to her car. As the engine turned over she reached inside her purse and grabbed a pain pill.

"Do not fear what you are about to be tested. Be faithful unto death, and I will give you the crown of life. Revelations two verse ten." Rhonda recited the bible verse out loud. She was extremely tired. This had been a very exhausting day. She drove home in silence, parked the car and walked straight to the bathroom to get a hot shower. Afterwards, she fell asleep. As she drifted off to the land of angels and dreams another Bible verse which she had learned as a child was in her thoughts.

If ye have the faith as a grain of mustard seed, ye shall say unto this mountain, move from here to yonder place; and it shall move; and nothing shall be impossible unto you. Matthew seventeen-twenty."

Chapter Eight

Today Rhonda was going to the shrink. She laughed to herself as she was dressing, because Joel had told her she needed one. She was crazy.

"Keep that thought Joel" she had said smugly. "A crazy woman can't possibly support herself! You will have your day ! The cup of justice will not pass you by forever."

She had phoned Dr. Mala the same day. Diedra had told her about a friend of hers that had gone there and found the therapy very soothing.

Rhonda had pondered about his name. Mala was the fictitious Bronze God of the Phoenicians in olden times. The Phoenicians had supposedly sacrificed their children to the big bronze belly of Mala in times of strife. They were expected to give up their most valuable possessions for their wish. Therefore, the innocent children were always given. Today, children are still betrayed. Only the method has changed as we as a society have become more civilized.

Not much has changed in hundreds of years. People still hurt and kill their children. But we have grown much more sophisticated. We now kill spouses or anyone that would dare to get in our way as well. So much for evolution!

Rhonda was on time today. It was exactly 10:00 A.M. when she was escorted into a large bright room with large colorful bouquets of flowers on all of the tables. A large uncluttered desk and two chairs were positioned near a large leather sofa but facing each other.

A medium built, dark, straight haired man held his hand out cordially while introducing himself. "I'm Dr. Mala. Pleasure to meet you. And you are?" He said without taking a breath.

"Rhonda Smith." Rhonda spoke almost defiantly.

"Sit down, please," he said easily as he moved one chair closer to the other and picked up a pad and pencil.

Rhonda noticed that he needed a hair cut and was not good looking. His casual attire of slacks, loafers and sweater did not seem very professional. He was younger than she expected.

Probably around thirty-five or forty she thought. She was not impressed and let him begin the conversation.

He casually picked up the notes his nurse had laid out for him. These notes included all of the questions and answers that she had asked Rhonda before the appointment had been scheduled.

Quickly reading the notes, Dr. Mala looked directly at Rhonda.

"Are you angry?" he asked.

"No," Rhonda said calmly but offering no more.

"Do you hate him, Rhonda?"

"Who him?"

"Your husband of course."

"Why? He had it all and gave it all up for a piece of…strange ass! You have the nerve to ask me if I hate him? My faith will not permit me to hate him or anyone else for that matter. But I do hate the things he does!"

"What about you?"

"I'm dispensable . . . just like everything else in his life."

"Do you have any respect left for him? Do you think you can still trust him?"

"No and no."

"Why are you here, Rhonda?"

"I guess… he finally convinced me that I have a black heart and am just a crazy bitch!" Rhonda said with no feeling or emotion. "I just wanted it confirmed by a professional."

"You don't have a black heart."

"How do you know? You don't even know me."

"What you have is a broken heart. There is a difference and as a professional I'm trained to recognize the differences."

"Right!" Rhonda answered curtly. Dr. Mala changed the subject.

"What do you think of our society and the rules for punishment?" he asked.

"What the hell does that have to do with anything?"

"I just would like to get an idea of how you think about things said."

"Society as a whole sucks. Everyone is busy trying to impress someone else and that someone else really doesn't give a damn. I think punishment laws are not extended into society as they should be."

"What do you mean?"

"Talk to any person on the street. Most people really believe if they have the money to buy the right attorney, any crime committed, even murder can be swept under the carpet!

Instead of meeting quotas and being so worried about what skin color people have, for example: are there three reds to five black and six whites? Better call in affirmative action. What is going to happen to our social status? Our legislators should address what kind of people we are."

"Like what?"

"I haven't decided if we should do it by vehicle color or house color but certain people in society should not have a color choice in what is the most visible possession they own. All whoremasters…should be forced to own only black cars, whores...red cars, child molesters...yellow cars, no choice given!

They would not be permitted to place their cars in a garage at home until after dark. Then, if you were hunting a place to live, you would know what kind of neighborhood you were driving through simply by the colors you saw. But, our society as a whole couldn't handle that. It's too simple. Or maybe it is as simple as legislating the color of all homes."

"Very interesting concept," Dr. Mala said emotionlessly. "Do you believe everything we are remembered for revolves around our choices or our actions?"

"Both," Rhonda answered. "A person's choices and actions affect everyone in their world."

"Emotional impacts cause us to repress feelings, and anger. We become depressed and freeze the anger. Everyone always refuses to address the real problem. David Seamandr had a book out for healing damaged emotions. It is very good. He calls depression frozen anger and I think he's right on target."

"My anger is not frozen, Dr. Mala. It's hot as hell. I read somewhere once that it is better to be hated for what you are than to be loved for something you're not. I actually believe that."

"But the past makes us what we are, Rhonda."

"Great! And I wear my Bitch Crown with pride. I learned early on if you think for yourself, make your own choices, are honest with everyone, face life straight on and just happen to be female you are crowned a crazy bitch. God help you if you're smart on top of that. I paid a huge price for my choices and no one ever cut me any slack. I'm not complaining. I am just telling you. We look out of different windows. Besides, I'll be divorcing myself from life soon anyway!"

"What do you mean by that, Rhonda? Are you thinking of suicide?"

"I wasn't, but if you want to go there we can."

"Do you sleep well?"

"Sometimes."

" Do you believe in God?"

"Certainly, do you?" Dr. Mala ignored the question and proceeded on. "What would you say would be the time in someone's lifetime that they would have the privilege of being closer to God then any other time in their life?" Rhonda pondered this question for a few seconds and then slowly started to speak. "I was with my mother in-law when she passed away…I guess for me it would be to…be there... and… to be permitted to have the experience of holding the hand of the person as God takes the other hand and quietly slips them from this world into the next." Dr. Mala never looked up, instead he continued to write and proceeded to the next question.

" When you should pass, what is the most important issue you are concerned about?"

"I have no pertinent concerns about the next world… my earthly concern is… I want my sons and their father to really love and care about each other. I want them to heal their wounds, forgive the past and to cherish the nice moments in their lives… I also want my sons to receive their rightful inheritance!" Rhonda laughed, trying to ease the moment. In First Timothy the fifth chapter eighth verse, it says: but if any provide not for his own and especially those of his own house…he hasth denied the faith and is worse than an infidel. Dr. Mala smiled, jotted something down and continued. " Do you love your husband?"

"You already asked me that question."

"I am asking it again." Rhonda remained silent for what seemed like an eternity. She began. "You know. I have asked myself that question at least a thousand times. Do I love him, or am I just dependent on him? Have both of us permitted issues to become so clouded and made the choice to just play the head games of always one upping the other never addressing the real issues at hand? Thinking about my life, in this instant, I would probably have to say I do love him." Feeling she had to qualify this answer she added. " If I didn't love him, I could not and would not have been hurt so much that my soul would bleed."

"How do you know if your soul bleeds?"

"Apparently you are one of the fortunates that has never had the capacity or ability to really feel that deeply about anyone or you would not be asking the question, Dr. If and when your soul ever begins to bleed, you will not have to ask anyone. Believe me. You will know!"

"I see here that you are going through a divorce. I would like to talk about that with you and perhaps discuss your independence."

"I'm really getting too tired to continue."

"We can cut this session short today if you like. I would like to see you next Friday. Shirley, uh, the nurse out in reception, she'll make an appointment for you on your way out."

"Yes, that would be better for me. I did not want to go where you were leading today anyway." Rhonda answered. "When my old friend, pain, arrives, I can't really think straight."

She was experiencing excruciating pain by now. Shirley was not at her desk. Rhonda hurriedly exited the building, proceeding directly to the car. When she arrived home she remembered C.J. was serving Joel the divorce papers today. Silently, she hoped Joel had received and taken the time to read the personal letter she had mailed. Her friend pain was going to make certain she would not be lonely tonight. The pain had never been this bad. It seemed to be getting worse by the minute. In silence, she reached for the bottle of pain capsules, walked slowly to the sink, filled a glass with water, placed two of the capsules in her mouth, drank the water, then slowly ascended the stairs to her lonely room.

She then went to bed.

Joe and Park arrived unexpectedly the next day and phoned Anna Mae, Rhonda's private nurse, to come in even though it was her day off. " Yes, she was available and would be glad to come right over."

Rhonda didn't seem good when they arrived that morning but refused to go to the hospital. "I want to be here at home in my own bed," she had said. And the pain was showing in her face.

Joel did get Rhonda's letter the prior day and also his divorce papers.

No one heard from him.

The letter read as follows:

My Dearest Joel,

I have finally learned a great lesson, too late I fear! Life is nothing but a series of hello's and goodbyes . . . forever in a state of change.

Many people pass through our lives; however, a few stay for a while. The one's you always remember in love have left their footprints on your heart. Some you have loved will leave only nasty heel marks, which have caused your soul to bleed. One fact remains constant and cannot be altered: <u>We are never the same again</u>!

When you chose to make a mockery of our marriage and place our family on your expendable list, you gave up respect and undying love. Once the vows have been broken the symbols have no meaning. That simple band of gold, suddenly became only an object to hide behind. All I ever wanted to know was, why? I just wanted to hear you say her name and tell me the truth. It would have helped me get through the pain you selfishly inflicted on me through no choice of my own. You chose to let us suffer and keep your allegiance to a stranger with her own agenda. She works to fill your every thought with commitment to everything and anything beyond family responsibilities and obligations.

Only you will have to face yourself in the mirror every day. At some point in your life, you will realize, no man lives only unto himself. You and she are both accountable. Good sex and love begin in the greatest sex organ God ever created; "The Mind!" You know, Joel, love is an action. It is not an emotion! When the time comes, Joe and Park will call for you to come home. Please don't disappoint them. You have in the past, by your actions and excuses. I have learned people are nasty to other people when they think that the other person doesn't like them or when the other person has found out what they truly are. You have worked with an unscrupulous element for so long that you became them. I truly hope you have taken the time to read this Joel. I wish you only happiness and truly hope you find what it is you have been searching for your entire life.

I thought you had it all; a wife that adored you and two wonderful sons who respected and loved you. Obviously, once again, I was wrong. I hope I have left a few footprints on your heart.

Once in awhile, if you're not careful, you can break something that can never be replaced or fixed. So please love and cherish the next girl in your life. Give her the respect and honor you so easily and joyfully took from me. And Joel, remember . . . some women are fragile. So handle with care. Perhaps you can give her what you were never capable of sharing with me . . . love, understanding, compassion. Everyone longs for the need to be loved and held and touched. I hope you can make her feel that she truly is someone special in your life. I always had to toot my own horn, which was something you always hated. I never felt like I was a special person to you. I knew deep down you would cause my soul to bleed one day, however, I stayed because I loved you so. I knew going in, I was expendable. Everything in your life always was. I always wished that I would not be! When the time came, I just did not know how to or have the strength to manage my losses. I am finding out that unmanaged pain and loss is literally killing me. If someone can't manage their losses, soon the losses will manage them. Parents with no self respect pass the same ideals on to their children . A good father or mother does not cheat! Your goal has always been to end up somewhere perfect with someone perfect. We all knew, everyone that is except for you. My hope is for you just end up someplace real. Take a good look at her, Joel. Is she really what she wants you to believe she is?

Is she worth it? I send this to you in love, Ronni.

When the letter arrived at Joel's office, Angie placed it on his desk, silently wondering if it was from Rhonda or Cassie.

Angie knew not to open anything for Joel that even looked remotely personal. She had done so once by accident and he had called her incompetent, telling her if it ever happened again she could seek employment elsewhere. Shortly after the letter incident, he had purchased a beeper, a car phone with voice mail on which only he knew the code to receive messages and an answering machine, just in case he was not there to get his calls. Angie had been forbidden to retrieve any messages for him. He no longer trusted her.

As Joel was going through the mail he suddenly noticed the pink envelope and recognized Rhonda's hand writing immediately. "Why doesn't that black hearted bitch give it a rest," he quietly said to himself as he opened the envelope?

He leaned back in the old oak chair which had once belonged to Rhonda's dad and began to read. When he came to the end he stood up, walked to the shredder and carefully shredded one sheet at a time. As he was going through the motions of paper to shredder his mind began to wonder.

He gazed around the large office with the dark gray carpet and oak furniture remembering Cassie, not Rhonda, behind those locked doors . . . making wild passionate love . . . not being able to keep his hands off of her body . . . getting drunk with her kisses. From this very office he had planned weekends with her, lied to Rhonda about working late and disappeared for drinks and sex. She called him constantly. And that damn Angie had the nerve to count the calls and tell Rhonda. She had even asked if there was a problem she could help with. When Joel asked why, she had looked him straight in the eye and said, "Well, Mr. Smith, I just wondered because that was call number thirty-four this week. Cassie would fax him in between calls and every chance they could steal he took her to a motel. Angie knew, because she still had access to the fax.

Cassie would call Rhonda to taunt her afterwards, but Joel would never believe it. Sometimes in life you only see and believe what you want to.

Rhonda had even told Joel about it. "Cassie says she often gets on top and presses your penis hard against her pussy . . . moving it back and forth, so she can get turned on. Actually she tells me you are a really lousy lover; however you're always more than willing to do anything she wants! She has you chained by your dick and you believe everything she tells you. She is delighted that you were so easy to snag. This is the filth verbatim that spills from that angelic mouth you hold so dear!"

"She would never say that!" Joel had screamed at Rhonda. "You, you black hearted bitch... you always want to make something that's beautiful ugly and dirty because you are jealous! She is no threat to you and would never do anything to hurt you!" Rhonda always had an answer. " I am the threat you fool! When I'm done, both of you will wish that you had never been born!"

When Rhonda followed him that next weekend, she confirmed for herself what liars and cheats' Joel and Cassie both were.

It says in the Bible "with knowledge comes great pain," and that sure was true. C.J. had talked Rhonda into going with him so she could see for herself. Rhonda received pictures of that weekend from C.J. The images would be forever stamped in her brain. Joel was lying on a bed and Cassie was laying on top of him on her back. Joel's eyes were closed and he was having the experience of his life, holding her breasts with his penis inside of her. By the time C.J. was finished filming with the small camcorder of some sort, he had what looked like a really first class porno film. She had sucked and kissed everything possible and he had reciprocated in kind. She had rubbed his penis back and forth near her sweet spot while laying on top of his gyrating body not letting him enter her while he moaned "Oh Baby" over and over. Rhonda had become physically ill and vomited every time she thought of it. C.J. seemed to actually enjoy watching the film which angered Rhonda because all she could do was cry. The feeling was like a great black pit in the deepest part of her soul that raged within. She was trapped in the center. It felt like hot coals from hell, an eternal fire that no one in this world would ever be able to extinguish!

Joel had lied again, but that was nothing new! His whole life was a lie. Rhonda had suddenly realized their life together was only a charade so Joel could have a public image and his own way. The fact was, he wanted it both ways.

Rhonda did not tell Joel until later that she had lied to him about there not being any pictures. She never told him that, in fact, she had a safety deposit box full of him with his women.

Rhonda had only said to him, "She may not be a threat to me Joel, but believe me. I am a threat to her! I possess everything necessary to make all of your wildest nightmares become reality!"

"You want her kids and family to hurt like you, you bitch! You don't care about anyone but yourself, Rhonda! That's what's wrong with you!"

"No one cared about me or my sons, Joel. Not even you. You're damn right! I'm not a bleeding heart for that whore of yours. And if I had photos I'd send the photos to her husband

and the other copies would be shown in court! I'd have everyone in Court, Jan, Cindy, Cassie . . . even you!

"You can't do that," he shouted back. "Check with your lawyer sweetie! I have rights too!"

"I did. I will have every one of your whores subpoenaed. And maybe I have pictures to prove my accusations after all. You can stand there like a circus ring master! You will have the time of your life!"

Joel arrived early at the house the next day. The first words out of his mouth were to inform Rhonda that Cassie had called him at the office. " So what else is new?" Rhonda had answered curtly. "She is so upset because someone called her husband and told him that you have some very interesting pictures he might like to see." He tried to remain calm as he spoke.

Joel was visibly shaken. " I told her that there were no pictures and nothing else, so not to worry!"

Rhonda became enraged. "Well guess what, lover? You should have checked with me! I have pictures on anything you want or could possibly think of! I even have action films! Ever hear of Daisy does Dallas? How does Cassie does Joel sound? Let's get one thing straight, Mr Smith. It will not be over until I say it is! So get a life ,Joel! I can prove my accusations after all. You have always told me I was crazy. You only forgot the most important thing. I'm not stupid and don't you ever forget it!" Why had this stupid note from Rhonda caused those thoughts to resurface? Joel found remembering things from the past that were distasteful bothered him. He would choose to busy himself with most anything. He had easily adapted to the practice of having no genuinely quiet time . He quickly learned if he kept busy enough, it was impossible for his mind to take him places he would rather not think about and therefore, make him uncomfortable with life.

Joel's mind snapped back to the present. *Maybe Rhonda was right. Cassie was using him.* But the thought passed as quickly as it came. She had told him about Rhonda's luncheon, but did not reveal the real reasons behind it. He had only laughed. " You have got to hand it to her anyway Cas, she has always been gutsy!" He had not pressured her to learn any more information about the luncheon. This had made Cassie a tad uncomfortable at the time. He never went there with Rhonda. She knew he would find out about it.

Rhonda had never been invited to come to Joel's office for any reason, He let her know early on, she was not welcome there. "You can always call Angie if you need me and she'll get in touch with me." He thought of this now. For an instant he felt a small pang of guilt.

Cassie often made regular trips to the office just to play with him. He loved it. Rhonda had known for a long time, secretly hoping, it would all turn out to be a big lie. There always seemed to be a problem that Cassie needed help with or she just had to see him. She never meant to fall in love with him, after all, she would never want to hurt anyone. She spent so much time blowing smoke up his anal canal and inflating his ego it was amazing to Rhonda that either was able to get any work done. The rumors were hot and heavy, as were the phone calls and the faxes. Having everything in place with C.J.'s help, there was not much Rhonda was not privy to. She did know that little things with Joel's work were suffering because Angie would call more often trying to reach him. Even a few irate clients had called the house.

Rhonda had never let onto Joel that she had known for a long time what he had reduced his life to.

Cassie had told her straight out she really didn't want Joel. She wanted job security. Through him, she could get the job she wanted or anything else for that matter. "Rhonda," she had said that day, "I just laid your ole man again. He's not that good in bed, honey. And I should know; I've had him plenty. When I'm through and get what I want, you can have the louse back. I certainly don't want to marry a liar and a cheat. You get his body back but I always keep their hearts and minds. I can't help it. Once they've had me no one else can compete! It'll be over when I say it is and not a day before. I'll get the job I want and let him think that he's dumping me. Tears and all, you know what I mean? But he will never be the same again. I suggest you dump him, Rhonda. A leopard never changes his spots and

Joel is always looking for a new conquest. Take it from someone who knows. I know men, better than almost anyone. Blow smoke up their ass, and massage their egos, act helpless and pretend you need them. You've got them then!. Believe me! If you just happen to get a divorce, I might marry him, just to keep him happy a little while longer. He is not poor. I know for sure because I checked. Know what I mean! I certainly don't plan to keep him around for the rest of my life. I ain't fucking nuts! There is too much age difference, and I sure as hell do not want to be saddled to some old man!"

Rhonda listened never answering back except to say "Thank you for sharing that with me Cassie!"

"Know what his favorite thing is Rhonda?" she had asked being very flippant. "He tells me to wear nothing at all. He thinks that's so cute and I play right along. Did he ever tell you that?"

With that, she hung up.

Joel had told Rhonda not to listen when people called to tell her things. He was so… kind. Right! The pain was so bad most of the time, it didn't matter anyway. Her self-esteem was all but gone. The pain from the cancer was getting to be almost more than she thought she could bear.

Let everyone have their fun. What's the point, anyway?

"He that endures to the end shall be saved" Matthew 10:22 Rhonda spoke softly as she lifted her eyes to the heavens on that day.

"Which one is going to be saved, Lord?" she added.

Once again there was only silence.

Chapter Nine

Joel's beeper went off. He made no move to check the number. An hour passed. Finally, he reached over, picked up the beeper and scrolled to look at the number. As he dialed the familiar number, he couldn't help but wonder why it was that she was bothering him for now. He was surprised to hear Park's voice on the line. "Come home now, Dad." Were the only words he said, before hanging up. There had been such urgency in the tone.

He left the office abruptly without a goodbye to a soul. The snow was falling lightly as he quickly drove to the house he had once called home.

When Joel arrived he went directly upstairs to be greeted by his sons and Anna Mae, Rhonda's nurse.

"Anna Mae just shook her head; her tearful eyes hardly acknowledged Joel. His son's barely spoke managing to choke out a small "Hi, Dad."

"Why wasn't I called sooner?" Joel spoke frantically while trying to suppress the anger with himself, for not phoning sooner.

"Right," Joe stated flatly.

"It's over Dad," Park managed to choke out. "You're too late. As always."

"But I was working," Joel said in an almost pleading manner.

"You haven't checked on her in weeks," Joe shot back. "You work twenty-four hours a day, Dad?"

"We know you have a tough schedule," Park interrupted, "with those women of yours and golf. But you're totally out of time. Guess what, Dad, Mom's out of time too!"

Joel ignored his sons as if they had not even spoken to him. *How dare they speak to me without respect* he thought for a second, but a memory of Ronnie's voice popped into his head. "Respect, trust, and love are all earned gifts, not given and taken for granted."

Joel opened the door to find his wife propped up in bed with lots of pillows and her grandmother's quilt pulled up around her. She looked almost like a small child in that humongous bed.

"Hi Ron" he tried to sound cheerful. "How's it going?" It took every bit of strength he could muster to smile and appear calm.

"Oh, hi Joel," Rhonda softly spoke back. "What are you doing here?"

"Park called me." Joel had regained his composure by now.

"Some party, huh?" Rhonda answered back. "Guess this is my last one, so I'm warning you Joel, don't rain on my parade." With that she tried very hard to laugh but could only smile.

Joel flashed his ever-famous smile that used to melt Rhonda's heart. Rhonda looked away as she fumbled trying to get something from the top of the night stand.

Joel reached over and picked up an envelope with his name on it. "This what you want?"

Rhonda nodded.

"What's this?" Joel asked, seemingly taken back.

"It's an action Joel," Rhonda said weakly. Her voice was getting weaker and she knew the angel of death was patiently waiting for her to finish. "Would you please leave now? I have finally taken care of everything here. I really must have a few minutes of private time with the man upstairs."

Joel turned slowly, clutching the envelope. As he reached the door, he turned looking straight at her. He tried to speak with tear filled eyes. "Ronnie," he managed to choke out, "I, I don't...I don't want you to die..." he tried to continue.

She did not let him finish but instead waved him out. "Go!" It was the only word she could utter.

Joel was now standing in the hallway holding the envelope. He slowly walked away and went down to the living room. He sat down on the white sofa and looked around the room. His thoughts drifted traveling back in time, the holidays, parties, graduations and the private moments. He recalled the times they had shared with their two sons together in this room. He closed his eyes and could see the boys opening Christmas presents and laughing. His mind traveled back to the time when Ronnie held

108

a huge party. The room full of people had played stupid fun games like Goose the Moose. The house had been so full of sounds and laughter then. The fourth of July parties had been the best around, fireworks, tons of food, adults and children everywhere. Ronnie always worked so hard to make sure everyone had a great time! His thoughts turned to the one man band. She always insisted on having him to play the music. He smiled remembering everyone dancing on the porch. There had been a lot of wonderful moments in this old house. This house held many happy memories.

His mind drifted to things back in time that had been long forgotten. " I wonder what happened to us? Now it's to late." He said quietly to Thor. The aging Doberman just raised his head at the sound of Joel's voice but did not get up.

He opened the envelope, which contained only a safety deposit box key and a brief hand written note as to what to do.

Rhonda's nurse was now by her side asking Rhonda if there was anything she wanted. Rhonda loved Anna Mae; in fact, she was the only nurse Rhonda had permitted access to her room during the last few days. The two of them had formed a special bond and shared many fears and secrets only the two of them would ever know. Anna Mae had just been told that she had terminal cancer also. She shared this secret with only Ronnie. Ronnie was crying softly ,desperately trying to hold back the tears. " I am not afraid of death, Anna Mae. Don't ever be afraid. I think the angel of death will just come and quietly slip each of us away when the man upstairs calls. It sure as hell can't hurt as much as living and trying to survive in this great big world," Rhonda now tried to smile as she spoke, looking up at her from the oversized bed.

"Please put on that CD by Celine Dion, I love so," Rhonda requested, barley able to whisper. "Please go down and get yourself a cup of tea and something to eat. I'll be just fine."

"But, I want to be here with you just in case you need me!" Anna Mae protested.

"I'll be OK," Rhonda lied. "Just hand me the Rosary and go on downstairs."

Anna Mae reluctantly did as requested. When she left the room she peeked back inside and could see Rhonda praying. Holy beads were now draped through her small hands. The music Rhonda requested was playing softly and Celine Dion's beautiful voice wafted throughout the house. Rhonda always loved the music system Joel had installed for her one Christmas. You could hear the music in every room . Each note rang out softly filling the air.

Joel got up from the sofa holding the note, upon hearing the footsteps on the stairs and followed Anna Mae to the kitchen. "I can't believe she threw you out too!" He tried to joke with his strained voice. Anna Mae didn't speak, only acknowledging Joel with a nod.

She and Rhonda often held many private conversations about life and death. Only she and Joe and Park knew that Rhonda had made her own funeral arrangements and there would be no public viewing. It was to be kept simple and quiet. The boys needed private closure on this part of their life. The day Rhonda had discussed this with them, Anna Mae had been present.

"I am making my own decisions on this," she had told them. "I feel your father gave up that right when he failed to live up to his wedding vows. He broke the Ten Commandments and his vows to me. I forgive him, but I will never ever forget," she told them calmly without malice. "Remember boys, when I'm gone, he is, and will always be your father! Even though he embarrassed you by his choices and caused you to lose respect for him, you both have got to learn that its okay to hate the choices he made but you must forgive. Sometimes you'll find in life that the one hardest to love may need your love the most. It is possible to hate what someone does but still love the person. Believe me and learn! This has been the most difficult lesson of my life. I know you were very disappointed and hurt by his choices . . . so was I. He is not alone. There are many people who never seem to learn. Sooner or later, one must live by the choices they make. Life is so fragile and precious! As long as everyone is alive there is always hope that things can be mended. But if one party dies, the chance of repair is lost forever. I beg you both not to waste your wounds. He will need your love more than ever now! No one ever gets out of this world totally unscathed. Every hurt you cause will come back to you ten fold but every good thing comes back seven times seven and more. God is very generous in many ways. Sometimes the ways can be so subtle that we forget to be thankful for what he has given us." Both of her sons listened to what she told them, never once breaking in on the conversation. Anna Mae had listened as intently as the boys, trying to absorb every word so she could recall this event at any given time in her mind.

As she sat and sipped her tea, sitting with Joel in silence, she was lost in thought , remembering that morning not so very long ago.

The music was playing softly, however, the words could be heard very clearly:

Close the door, shut the world away.
All the fights gone from this wounded heart.
Across the floor dreams and shadows play like wind blown refugees.
Call the man who deals in love beyond repair.
He can heal the world of hearts in need of care.
Shine a light ahead when the next step is unclear.
Call the man he's needed here.
I close my eyes; I remembered when your sweet love filled this empty room.
The tears I cry won't bring it back again unless the lonely star should fall.
Call the man who deals in love beyond repair.
He can heal the world of hearts in need of care.
Shine a light ahead when the next step is unclear.
Call the man he's needed here.
Needed in the chaos and confusion from the plains to city hall.
Needed where the proud who walk the wire are set to fall.
Call the man who deals in once upon a time.

Maybe he can mend this broken heart of mine.
Shine a light ahead.
Now the future isn't clear.
Call the man he's needed here.
Call the man he's needed here[11].

In Rhonda's head, the man she always called was God. She was having her final conversation with him now.

The first part of the note held instructions about the safety deposit box and personal property. The next page was a short personal note to Joel. He sat quietly reading the brief personal note over and over. When the music stopped he jumped as if he had been suddenly jolted by a bolt of electricity.

The note read:

My Dearest Joel,

You really <u>do</u> need God in your life. You'll find out sooner or later that "No man lives only unto himself." The greatest love of all is never ending. Only God can give that to you.

I have stood by myself in the lonely desolation in which anger, hurt, betrayal and illness have placed me . . . through no choice of my own. But that is life; a series of events that happen often through no choice of our own. You made me believe I was insane for doubting you.

Well Joel, I'm not insane, you see! Someone of real quality wants me now.

His name is God. I hope someday I'll get to introduce you.

If you're reading this letter it means I didn't get to kick your butt in court. I really would have, you know! Reality is what it is. My life did not turn out

---

[11] Artist, Celine Dion from Falling Into You Written by Andy Hill & Pete Sinfield

to be what I wanted it to be. Somewhere along the way, we lost something impossible to ever get back. I learned grief really has no rules.

We both blew it this time around.

I cry, only for things that will never be. Hopefully the man upstairs is saving my tears to light the heavens for you and the boys at night.

God put you in my path and me in yours for a reason! I do truly believe that everything under heaven has a purpose. But did we learn the lesson being taught?

I wonder if there really are malls in hell? And if there are, I wonder if you'll be managing one of them. Tell Marti and Diedra if there's a way, I'll let them know!

It's time to say goodbye. And, you know, the journey wasn't all bad. We almost had it all. Almost!

I wish you love.

Ronnie

As quickly and abruptly as the music had stopped, Rhonda was gone! There was no fanfare…only silence, nothing at all! Rhonda just slipped away. Like she had often done in life. Her time to live had passed. It was her time to die. Joe and Park were at her side holding her hand, in the same instant God took her other hand to lead her into the world beyond.

When Joel entered the room he bent over and gently kissed her forehead and closed her eyes. No one spoke.

Park tearfully kissed his mother as did Joe and left the room. Joel sat down on the old nursing rocker, a rocker that had never been removed from the bedroom since the boys were born.

"It's an antique," she had said long ago. "We can't get rid of it. After all, it was your grandmother's." The sound of her voice echoed in his ears.

He looked around the old familiar room that once was so full of life. Now it seemed suddenly so cold and silent. On the dresser he spotted the poem by D. H. Lawrence she had framed so many years ago, called *Self Pity*. He silently read the poem to himself, placed it back and left the room, softly closing the door behind him.

Self Pity by D.H. Lawrence

> ***"I never saw a wild thing feel sorry for itself***
> ***a sparrow frozen and falling from a broken bough***
> ***Never felt sorry for itself."***

There was no public viewing as Rhonda requested. The boys spent a final few minutes at the casket alone and kissed for the last time the lifeless corpse which had once held the spirit of their mother. Joel was now standing between his two grown sons, bent over the casket. His lips lightly touched Rhonda's cheek. He was visibly shaken. It was the first time in their entire lives his sons had seen him cry.

"Sorry, Rhonda. I never meant to hurt you," he whispered between the agonizing tears. "You were always one hell of a lady! Guess that's why I loved you so. It's too late to tell you all I want to say. If you can hear me, I . . . I found my way back home."

"Come on, Dad," Park said quietly. "We've got to wind things up here. Father Bill wants to start the mass on time."

"She was right, you know?" Joel spoke softly to Park.

"Right about what?"

"No man lives only unto himself."

The church was full by the time Joel and the boys entered for the service. The music Ronnie had chosen made the mass seem more like a celebration, than a funeral. Father Bill reminded everyone that it was indeed a celebration, a celebration of Rhonda's new life with God. When he finished the homily, he did not proceed directly to the next part of the mass. Instead he

114

picked up a piece of paper and looked up at the congregation. "This is a poem that Rhonda asked me to read at her funeral. It is her gift to each of you that knew and loved her. The name of the poem is, "When Tomorrow Starts Without Me, By David Romano."

When tomorrow starts without me,
And I'm not there to see:
If the sun should rise and find your eyes,
All filled with tears for me;
I wish so much you wouldn't cry,
the way you did today,
while thinking of the many things,
we didn't get to say.

I know how much you love me,
As much as I love you,
And each time that you think of me,
I know you'll miss me too;
But when tomorrow starts without me,
please try to understand,
that an angel came and called my name'
And took me by the hand,
she said my place was ready,
in heaven far above,
And that I'd have to leave behind,
All those I dearly love.

But as I turned to walk away,
a tear fell from my eye,
for all life, I'd always thought,
I didn't want to die.
I had so much to live for,
so much yet to do, it seemed almost impossible,
that I was leaving you.

I thought of all the yesterdays,
the good ones and the bad,

I thought of all the love we shared,
And all the fun we had.

If I could relive yesterday,
just even for a while,
I'd say goodbye and kiss you
And maybe see you smile.

But then I fully realized,
that this could never be,
for emptiness and memories would take the place
of me.

And when I thought of worldly things,
I might miss come tomorrow,
I thought of you and when I did,
my heart was filled with sorrow.

But when I walked through heaven's gates,
I felt so much at home.
When God looked down and smiled at me,
from His great golden throne,
He said " This is eternity ,
And all I've promised you.

Today for life on earth is past,
but here it starts anew.
I promise no tomorrow,
but today will always last,
And since each day's the same day,
there's no longing for the past.

You have been so faithful,
so trusting and so true.
Though there were times you did some things,
you knew you shouldn't do.
You have been forgiven
And now at last you're free.

> **So won't you take my hand**
> **And share my life with me?"**
> **When tomorrow starts without me,**
> **don't think we're far apart.**
> **For every time you think of me,**
> **I'm right there, in your heart.**

Father Bill quietly laid the paper down, paused for a moment and asked everyone to rise for the profession of faith. The mass continued as usual. The communion song she had chosen was "On Angels Wings." It certainly was not a depressing melody. At the end of the mass , just before everyone exited the church, everyone joined in to sing "How Great Thou Art."

It was indeed a celebration!

Chapter Ten

The boys told Marti as soon as they picked her up at the airport.

Marti called Diedra and C.J. called Marti. Each seemed surprised. Everyone loved the ad.

"Ronnie is still with us," Diedra had told Marti. "Do you think she set this up before . . . ?" Her use of the word 'before' was obvious, trying to evade the death issue.

"Most likely," Marti answered, chuckling to herself. "Or maybe C.J. did it for her. I'm going to try to call him again."

When Marti reached C.J. he was the first to mention the ad. "Great ad, Marti!" he had said. "Ronnie will make them all pay, even from hell, if she's not too busy at the malls. When did you two set that up? Very clever! I never would have thought of it."

"Come on, C.J. Admit you did it," Marti laughingly chided him.

"Yeah, Marti, sure. Who are you kidding? You probably did it yourself. Diedra was the only person Ronnie ever confided in except you and me, and I sure as hell didn't do it. There is an outside chance that Diedra did it."

"Diedra called me," Marti shot back, "I didn't do it, nor did she. Besides, Diedra is too nice to ever do such a thing. I actually think she believes Ronnie did it somehow."

They both laughed, each silently blaming the other, wishing they had the foresight to do it themselves.

Six months later Diedra ran into Joel at the supermarket. With him was a tiny blue-eyed blonde. She sort of reminded her of Rhonda ,in a strange way.

Diedra just couldn't contain herself any longer.

"Hi Joel," she spoke cheerily to him. "And this must be the ad lady!"

"No one answered," Joel spoke hurriedly without smiling.

"I should think not!" Diedra spoke back haughtily, blushing at the same time, wondering what would ever make her say such a thing.

"This is Sheila Johnson," Joel spoke easier now. "May I present the illustrious Diedra Kane, a close friend of my deceased wife." They exchanged a small greeting and Diedra hurriedly excused herself. As soon as she arrived back at home, her finger was dialing Marti. As she was telling the story to Marti, a cold chill came over them . Both thought of Rhonda. Each was thinking *Ronnie won the battle but died before she had a chance to win the war*. She always was like a breath of cold, chilling air and just as unpredictable. The ad would prove to be the talk of the town for many months to come.

"Adultery and disease are not respecters of class, age or race," Rhonda had told them both one afternoon which now, seemed so long ago. "I really must be the queen of the chosen women! And what a bargain I got; three for the price of one! You've got to admit. I always was very lucky!" Ronnie had always looked out of a different window than anyone else and sometimes the strangest things had amused her. They had just shaken their heads and laughed with her.

The ad read:

PROFESSIONAL MALE SEEKS NEW WIFE!

WWM in search of ... The Perfect Woman

One white single woman age 30-40 to marry. Must be able to paint and paper walls, do laundry, clean house, wash windows, clean screens, put in storm windows. Willing to iron, cook delicious low fat meals, and wash dishes. Must be able to sew, grocery shop, and have interior decorating abilities, pick up mail and take out garbage.

Will reheat meals when I am late, which is often.

Must not be overweight, always smiling and laughing. No history of mood swings and a nonsmoker. No children please! Must always be

dressed attractively, manicured and willing to sign a pre-nuptial agreement .

You will be required to present a written health certificate from your doctor attesting to the fact that you are in the best of health. Over the age of 40 need not apply. Must be able to entertain yourself and be emotionally stable. I golf, watch football, wrestling <u>and</u> only I choose the music played whenever I am home. I will pay for you to get your hair done once a month, style cut and blown dry . . . not to exceed $50.00. Included will be hospitalization, room and board and a stipend for personal necessities. You may ask no questions about my job or what I do with my time. The pre-nuptial states: the arrangement may be terminated due to illness. Complaints about being tired or nagging will not be tolerated. Career oriented females may feel free to apply. All applicants will be considered. You will always project the perfect marriage to the public and under no circumstances challenge, complain or disagree with me.

All handwritten applications will be considered for an interview. No phone calls, please.

Please respond immediately by mail.

"Applications are due by March 10. Please include a self-addressed stamped envelope. You will be notified by mail as to when an interview is to be granted.

Submit to:
Mr. Joel Smith
893 Lake Port Road
Newton Falls, Mo. 01968-0427

One Month After Rhonda's Funeral:
The Day of the Ad

Exactly one month to the day, the one-page personal ad appeared in all local papers.

Ironically, four households received personal notes with one picture of each of Joel's female companions with him in precarious positions. The photos had been carefully placed inside each folded note.

Joel was furious when he opened the morning paper and spotted the ad. "Who would do such an evil thing?" He spoke out loud, screaming to no one but the dog. He immediately phoned one of the papers and asked for the party that handled personal ads.

"Mary speaking. How can I help you today? We are running a special this week. Five lines for . . . "

Joel interrupted trying to sound calm and unruffled. "This is Joel Smith. A personal ad appears on page forty-two today which has my name and address inserted for the responses. Someone has made a significant error. I am quite upset about this. My dear wife passed away only one month ago today. If this is a joke, I certainly don't find any humor in this tasteless ad."

"One moment please," Mary stated clearly, trying to sound concerned. "I'll check that for you."

Joel sounded demanding and quite annoyed. "I want to know exactly who placed the ad and who paid for it? I swear, someone's head is going to roll over this!"

In a few minutes', Mary was back on the line. "Mr. Smith, the ad was placed yesterday morning by a Rhonda K. Smith, your address and phone number. It was paid for in cash and was to run for today only."

"What did this person look like? Who placed the ad?" Joel asked.

"Mr. Smith," Mary sounded somewhat put out now. "We take hundreds of ads daily. This one was taken by phone yesterday and held until someone dropped off the money. The envelope was dropped off and placed on my desk in the early afternoon. The envelope was typed on the outside. I do recall the envelope as it was pale pink with the name Rhonda Smith. I noted that the envelope had the same address as appears in the ad. When I opened it, there was only cash inside, which I deposited, and cleared the account."

"Thank you," Joel said politely and hung up the phone.

He called Angie at the office to say he wouldn't be in, telling her to cancel his appointments.

"Have you seen the morning paper?" Angie asked without thinking.

"I sure as hell have! I'm sure everyone in four counties has seen it! If I ever find out who did this, their ass is grass!" he yelled angrily as he slammed down the phone.

He brooded the morning away trying to figure out who would do such an awful thing. He had never really hurt anyone that mattered. The women he fooled around with knew he was married! They got what they wanted and so had he. No one was hurt. Well, no one except Ronni, rest her soul, and she was gone now.

In the early afternoon, Joe and Park walked in together each holding a copy of the daily paper. Park also held today's mail in his hands. He handed it all to his father.

Joe spoke first. "How's it goin' Dad?"

"Okay," Joel smiled at his name sake while speaking.

"Guess you saw the paper?" Park spoke with no emotion.

"Yes Park. I saw it. Go figure! Who could be so crass?" Joel rambled. "After all, we've been through?"

Joel immediately held out a letter that was addressed to his boys. Park took hold of it and opened it, reading the text quickly. He handed it off very quickly to Joe saying, "You need to read this."

My Dearest Joe and Park,

Always remember, it's not what you have in your life, but who is in your life that's most important! The people hardest to love are the ones that need your love the most, so fill your life with love and laughter and always

remember to be careful of your choices. When you hurt the people that love you, those hurts have a strange way of creeping back into your own life. Please don't waste your wounds. With each wound you waste a light goes out in Heaven . . . and you know how I hate the dark! My hope is that your lives are filled with love and will always be a festival of lights, both day and night.

Love always,
Mom

Joel didn't ask Joe about the letter he was reading, but it evidently was affecting him emotionally. As Joe finished the letter, Park started joking with his father. "Well, Dad, there's only one person we know with enough guts to do something like this . . . making reference to the ad as he picked up the paper, and she's gone. We never knew anyone as gutsy as Mom. I'll bet she's giving the angels a run for their money, or the devil." He was obviously trying to make light of how much he missed his mother.

Joe and Park both laughed and Joel smiled. They'll be all right, he thought. *We did one thing right, Ronnie.*

"We can order in for lunch if you haven't eaten," he said to the boys.

"Let's order pizza and put on a movie," Joe said.

"You or Park can order. I want to go through the mail."

Joel sat down still holding the mail. A small pink envelope fell to the floor. Park picked it up and looked at Joe.

"Looks like mom's stationery," Joe said.

"It's hers," Park said, his voice shaking. "It has her inscription on it!"

"Must be a wrong address on it?" He took the envelope from Park turning it over, expecting to see the return 'wrong address' or 'postage needed' stamp. Instead, it was addressed neatly to him in the handwriting of his deceased wife.

"What the . . . ?" Joel stopped. It was Rhonda's stationery! The top gold embossed familiar inscription read *From the desk of Rhonda Jean Smith* . . . The handwriting was definitely hers.

He sat down. His large hands were trembling as he slowly proceeded to open the small pink envelope. The note fell from the envelope, gently floating to the floor. He quickly bent down, picked it up and began to read.

The brief note read:

My Darling Joel,

You were right about one thing. It's not how you play the game. It's whether you win or lose! <u>Everyone</u> remembers the winner! And so, my love, read today's paper!

> **Game over!**
> **I win!**
> **Gotcha!! I win!! Love to you!!**
> **XO-Ronnie**

Joel started laughing and shook his head. He handed the note to Joe and Park. Each quickly read the note and looked at their Dad.

"She always did have to have the last word." Joel said in near shock.

"She played to win!" Joe said proudly with a grin.

"Well, she won round one, didn't she Dad?" Park said, smiling at his father.

"Yes she did!" Joel answered with a smile. "But I'll bet you both, Marti helped her."

"No way!" Joe spoke up. "Aunt Marti's in France. She won some contest and has been gone for a week. Park and I have to pick her up at the airport tomorrow night."

Early that same morning, a certain attorney stopped to pick up the morning paper and a cup of coffee. This was the usual routine practiced by him on the days when he was working at his office. Alone in his office, he calmly sat down at his desk and opened the local paper to the ads. He read the ad and laughed. For the longest time he just sat alone in the silence and slowly sipped the coffee, occasionally glancing at the ad and smiling to himself. He never mentioned the ad to a soul and no one ever in their wildest dreams even associated him with it.

Each of Joel's three close female friends received the same embossed stationery with pertinent pictures enclosed and a brief note.

If you are reading this note, then I have died. I hope you enjoy the picture of you and Joel as much as you enjoy the ones of him with your competition.

Everyone pays for their choices in life. Andrew Carnegie always said. "I pay no attention to what a man says, I watch what he does." Good advice, don't you think!

I apologize for dying so abruptly but it is only God that holds the keys to hell and death.

By my death, God has so quickly taken you from judgement to mercy!

My hope for each of you is that you will expend the energy used that hurt my children, myself, and others to draw your own nearer to your heart. If this can be done, nothing endured has been without purpose. Hopefully it will serve to bring everyone involved closer to their faith in some small way.

It is my fervent hope that you will renew your friendship with the man upstairs! I call him God!

Always,
Rhonda J. Smith

Post Script

I would like to thank God for giving me the ability to tell you this story about a chosen woman. I would also like to thank my husband and sons for their encouragement and support, my parents for the help with research and also family, friends and women who were willing to share very painful moments and feelings with me.

Without the information I collected, Rhonda Smith could never have existed for any of us. Parts of Rhonda lie somewhere deep in each of us. You'll recognize her when you take the time to listen. Each of us will have many hard choices to make during our life on this planet. To me, the most important part of living is being able to look back once in awhile, if only for a brief second, and know in my heart, without question, the decisions I made were the right ones. What if this life is only a test for the next one? I believe we will be tested over and over again, therefore, the victory does not come in death but in how we govern our personal lives!

May the words on Rhonda's tombstone remind each of us of what we are, who we are, what we have become and where we are going.

Rhonda J. Smith
March 28, 1941 - January 4, 1997

Who can find a virtuous woman? for her price is far above rubies.
Proverbs 31:10

ABOUT THE AUTHOR

Retha Sullivan is a fifty-nine-year-old homemaker. She lives in a small middle-class suburb of Pittsburgh, Pa. With her husband Jack and Carlie, her Doberman. She has owned and operated a home based textile printing business for fifteen years and also co-owned a small gift shop for a short time. Mrs. Sullivan served on the local library board for three years, and has taught arts and crafts at the nearby community college. She enjoys painting, writing, stock market investing, reading, and riding a motorcycle with her husband, accessing the internet, and exchanging ideas with her friends, clients, and her family which includes two grown sons, Jack and Patrick.

"I am a firm believer that most events in life are caused by choice rather than change. Choices cause change! I encourage my readers not to become complacent and apathetic. The time will come when each of us must stand up and be counted for what we believe in!"